Imaginary Parents

IMAGINARY

ARENTS

text by **Sheila Ortiz Taylor**
art by **Sandra Ortiz Taylor**

University of New Mexico Press
Albuquerque

Library of Congress
Cataloging-in-Publication Data

Taylor, Sheila Ortiz, 1939-
Imaginary parents/text by
Sheila Ortiz Taylor;
art by Sandra Ortiz Taylor.
— 1st ed.

p. cm.

ISBN 0-8263-1727-8 (cl)
ISBN 0-8263-1763-4 (pa)

1. Taylor, Sheila Ortiz, 1939-
— Childhood and youth.
2. Women authors,
American—20th century
— Family relationships.
3. Los Angeles (Calif.)
— Social life and customs.
4. Family—California
— Los Angeles.
I. Taylor, Sandra Ortiz, 1936-
II. Title.

PS3570.A9544Z467 1996
813'.54—dc20
[B]   95-50175
CIP

Art work photographed by
Philip Cohen

Designed by Sue Niewiarowski

Many people have helped me in my work. I would particularly like to thank my companion Joy Lynn Lewis, my dear friends Juan Bruce-Novoa, Nancy Sternbach, Monifa Love, Ed Love, my cousin Terry Ann Fox, and the graduate students in my Latina Fiction Seminar. I am also grateful to John Wingler for his kindness in letting me wander through my ancestral house in Los Angeles and to my cousin April Fox for letting me include her essay "Requiem for Mymama" in this work.

The art work was partially funded by a grant from the Money For Women/Barbara Deming Memorial Fund, Inc. Warm thanks to Pam McAllister and the Board of Directors for believing in this project and for their years of support and encouragement to women writers.

Several of these chapters appeared elsewhere, and I extend grateful acknowledgment to editors and publishers. "Photograph #2," "Dinner 1945," and "Dinner 1948" appeared in *Sun Dog: The Southeast Review;* "La Frontera" in *Two Worlds Walking* (New Rivers Press); "Pocadillas," "And the Skies Are Not," "Convoy," and "The Birthday Party" in *Americas Review;* "Esther Williams' Sister" in *Innisfree;* and "Hearts" in *Chicana Criticism and Creativity: New Frontiers in American Literature.*—*Sheila Ortiz Taylor*

A nest—and this we understand right away—
is a precarious thing, and yet it sets us to daydreaming
of security. And so when we examine a nest, we place
ourselves at the origin of confidence in the world,
we receive a beginning of confidence, an urge toward
cosmic confidence.

GASTON BACHELARD

CONTENTS

LA GALERÍA
BOOK THREE

LIST OF ILLUSTRATIONS

Descriptive annotations by Sandra Ortiz Taylor

Texas Two-Step/History of a Self-made Man. Interior. /*146*

Since our grandfathers on both sides of our family were craftsmen, I was drawn to this rusted toolbox as a potential container for a family chronicle. My father once told me that after his dad's death he came home one night and saw my grandfather's overalls hanging in the garage and burst into tears. Somehow this battered toolbox, its appearance suggesting so much history, made this recollection vivid. And so I chose it to contain my memory of my father's story of his odyssey from a small town in Texas to Los Angeles. He transformed himself from an impoverished working-class background to become both a successful studio musician and a practicing attorney, the latter profession nearly killing him. He made his final transformation, while still a musician, by completing the building of an offshore sailboat, learning navigation, and becoming captain of our family crew.

"You Think Too Much" /*150*

This was a bit of family wisdom contributed by my mother during our formative years.

LA GALERÍA

Girl's Dream /*165*

Part of our family history included my father mercilessly teasing my little sister about wanting a horse. Little did any of us recognize the horse was Pegasus. My childhood ambition was to be an artist and hers to be a writer.

Homage to a Tree House /*166*

This scene is a miniature stage, an image appropriate to our activities of performing make-believe scenarios. Nowhere was composite imagination more active than in our "Electricity Tree," a magical powerplace.

Night Closet /*167*

My sister's Robin Hood hat and vest appear in our closet. All the nighttime fears disappear as the imaginary landscape takes their place.

Good Dog/Bad Dog /*168*

This piece concerns a traumatic childhod event in which my worst fears came true; a lesson in learning to trust one's instincts ("Don't be afraid, he won't hurt you").

Cowgirls Don't Wear White Gloves. Interior. /*169*

Winifred, Her Story. Interior. /170

Winifred lived and died before our feminist movement. Part of our motivation for telling her story comes from the lack of perspective we had, being children, at the time of her dramatic death. Now, as mature women who have felt the influence of feminism, we have formed a very different scenario from the one that the family told. All the family snapshots in which Winifred appeared were torn to eliminate her visage. I hope in some small way we are restoring her image.

My Mama's Mexi-Briefcase. Interior. /171

The age and pattern of this case instantly evoked grandmother Ortiz and at the same time made me recall my childhood fascination with our dad's briefcase. In her briefcase is her life, *vida,* her family, *familia.*

As children she used to invite us, a special treat, into the inner sanctum of her cramped bedroom to view her miniature collections. We were in awe of this room, filled with holy pictures, painted plaster saints, and flickering votive candles. She stood us on a chair to see the glass shelves which held the menagerie —*pocadillas,* as she would say—which was excelled only by her collection of curious succulents and cacti. She would conduct tours of these wonders, telling us names and sources of strange natural forms.

Her only contribution to the family's front garden was an astonishing hedge of enormous aloes. When one of her grandchildren was injured by their thorns, she cut them all off with her dressmaking shears. The tortilla in the piece is her biological clock; she gave birth to thirteen babies and had eleven living offspring. She stands proudly before one of her enormous aloe plants with my sister and me and one of our cousins. She was the *corazón,* the heart of her family, but apart from this context, I realize that I never knew her. She remains to me, as she appeared in so many snapshots, a shadow, yet a powerful maternal presence.

Recuerdos Para Los Abuelitos /172

Inscription: "Seven months after her virgin has taken her from him—his wife of so many years—he lies in their bed and dreams of his own death." My grandfather took his own life shortly after he lost my grandmother. The shotgun that he will use is beside him. My family had a disturbing tendency to merge so totally in partnerships that the death of one would create a void so great as to endanger or even destroy the other.

My grandfather's choice, carried out in the family home, with other family members present, completed the destruction of the family which had begun with the death of my grandmother.

Catch the Wave /173

My father's dream in process. At the base of this piece, the hull of his boat dwarfs his young daughters. His musical instruments are evoked, as well as something of the fearsomeness of the experience of sailing on the open sea as a family.

El Músico y la Dama. Interior. /174

This *caja* (box), the musician and the Lady/ Woman, is the most narrative of the twenty-five family pieces I have done. Figures from the *Lotería,* a traditional Mexican game of chance, become my parents at their meeting. The romantic aura they weave about their relationship permeates and animates this piece. The *corazón* card is of special significance in the futures of our family. My father's first heart attack hung like a shadow over our daily lives (the prognosis being a slim five years left to live). My father's dream (realized in his post heart attack life) of an offshore sailing boat brought us closer together, navigating the channel to Catalina Islands each summer.

Fly Away /175

Exotic woman with a hibiscus in her hair, needing to keep her children in the nest.

House of Pictures. Interior. /176

An *ofrenda* to the days of childhood. There are two areas of text printed in the lid, suggesting that the box is a treasure trove within a narrative. The first text is spoken by the image of the bird: "I sing the pictures of the book and see them spread out: I am an elegant bird for I make the codices speak within the house of pictures" (Náhuatl poet). The second is the quotation from Gaston Bachelard quoted at the beginning of this book. The lid's exterior has elements that represent time congruent with the narrative as well as the future.

Ofrenda for a Maja /177

In "*Ofrenda* for a *Maja*"(offering, tribute, memorial for a charismatic woman), I was able to chronicle my mother's life before and after my father's death, using miniature objects, sculpting, painting, and collaging. I recreated our family patio with her sunglasses on the table; she has just sat down to have her cigarette. The broom is waiting for her to resume her constant labors. Only with the death of my father does she begin to emerge as a self-defining individual. She demonstrated her new-found independence by embarking on a solo voyage of discovery.

Pelorus /178

The pelorus "is used to determine bearings of charted objects (buoys, towers, lighthouses) so that the boat's position may be determined." This piece, the last in the cycle, celebrates a lifelong collaboration.

FOREWORD

Reader,

This book is made of bones. *La Huesera,* Bone Woman, crouching over the bones of the dead coyote, sings them back to life. I crouch over the bones of my parents, remembering and transforming. I strike attitudes, postures of innocence, reverence, amusement, anger, tenderness, mirth, fury. I accept what comes and the order in which it comes. All the ghosts that rise up are mine. I claim them. I am dancing with death.

Call this book autobiography. Or memoir. Call it poetry. Call it nonfiction. Or creative nonfiction. Call it the purest fiction. Call it a codex. Give it a call number.

I say it is an altar, an *ofrenda.* Small objects with big meaning set out in order. Food, photographs, flowers, toys, *recuerdos,* candles. *Pocadillas,* my grandmother would say. Scissors and paste, my father would say. *Bricolage,* my sister says. A miniaturist to the bone, Bone Woman insists on all the parts.

La Huesera. Who else am I, in this making?

A lawyer, like my father. I question, I return to the scene of the crime, search for weapons, motives, opportunities. I assemble the witnesses in the drawing room. And yet I cannot interrogate them; I can only heap up evidence.

I am a diver, too. Not in wet suit, mask, tank, knife. No, the kind of diver called from the village because she is known for her skill at swimming, because everybody knows this woman is running toward the river even before she has been told of the drownings. She is methodical. She swims back and forth across the river in an intricate pattern, her head disappearing below the surface, then reappearing. She is patient. Finding nothing, she begins a new pattern, one intersecting at different angles the old one. She is as committed to finding the drowned ones as if they were her own parents.

Call me Coyote too, driving my Selves too fast in weather too hot, through ambiguous zones of time, gender, and race with all the windows down. When you ask for my papers I hand you this book.

This book you hold, this *ofrenda,* like all altar art and most rescue work, was not realized in solitude. My sister and I have collaborated in this piece. She created the visual art and I wrote the text, though much of my writing was inspired by our conversations and mutual re-collections as we cooked together or dreamed our way through boxes of family photographs. In our working we did not try to make art and text replicate each other but rather to refract, casting new shadows, throwing new angles of light. While our individual memories always differed, we learned to value this difference and to use it as a way of layering our work. What remained constant and steadfast—in addition to a lifelong friendship—was our common vision of our parents as handsome, intriguing, perhaps unknowable people whose love affair with each other and with the strange southern California culture of the war years shaped them and us in ways we wanted to explore, critique, and celebrate with each other and with you.—*Sheila Ortiz Taylor*

ART NOTES

Much of my work is related to family history. My motivation partially comes from a need to try and understand my parents and our lives together and how that past continues to influence the present tense of both my sister and myself.

Our parents were handsome, attractive people, even by Hollywood standards. I think my sister and I grew up a little in awe of our glamorous progenitors (I think of my mother as the Dolores Del Rio of L.A.'s Silver Lake district). They had come from poor working-class family backgrounds and they were determined not to duplicate the lives of their parents. They managed, together, to live out the American Dream, Southern California style. It was as if they invented themselves. It is no wonder that we are participants in their myth. Through our art forms, we are now their shadowmasters.

My mother provided us with a diverse, large, extended family. Our grandmother Ortiz, known to us as "Mymama," had produced eleven children so our nuclear family of four frequently merged with dozens of cousins, great aunts and uncles as well as our mother's cast of brothers and sisters. To sit in Mymama's kitchen was to hear stories being told in both English and the song-like cadence of the Spanish that Mymama used to speak to her sisters. All of this was accompanied by the staccato sounds of Mymama's brown soft hands as she slapped the tortillas into shape for the griddle. This may be the origin of our strong narrative proclivities. I certainly was drawing then, and my grandmother was my archivist, saving my work "until you will appreciate it."

My sister's partner said, perceptively, that she regarded the art for *Imaginary Parents* as a separate but parallel narrative to the text, that the texts intertwined like the double helix. I liked that image and felt the truth in it.

The viewer/reader may note that I frequently make use of what in art parlance is referred to as a "found object." These objects may stimulate the concept of a piece, such as the antique miniature Robin Hood hat and vest that became part of "Night Closet." Later, when I described the piece to Sheila, she responded that it was her hat. She helped me recall that as a child she prevailed on our mother to sew her such a hat, replete with a feather, that she wore daily at play. No wonder I was drawn to it.

When I work with boxes as "found objects" they may be containers for pieces. As such I frequently regard them as books; that is, the outside is the cover that sets the mood for the interior action.

People frequently ask me if I visualize a whole piece before I begin to work. I usually don't have a total concept, and half the fun is the discovery that comes along with the process. In particularly successful pieces there are layers of meaning, like letters from the unconscious waiting to be opened.

While I do not plan out any single piece of work, still I know I have been working toward this collection for a long time. Fifteen years ago I wrote in my journal words that seem to anticipate the spirit and even the form of *Imaginary Parents:*

"When we were small, time moved in an arc above us. We

may have noticed it, but we never watched it. Days were full, rich in sights, smells, sounds, and adventure. Adventure, whenever the adult world was absent. The smallest circumstance pricked our curiosity. We were at once explorers and experimenters. There was no field that didn't give way to our persistence: biologists among the bugs and butterflies; botanists among the early spring wildflowers; collectors of nearly everything. For beauty took many forms. A wondrous catalogue of objects: a lovely bird's egg, a shed reptile skin, discards from trash cans. We equipped a tall tree with the plunder of a radio buff's trash. There were switches, tubes, mysterious objects—all becoming part of the power of The Electricity Tree. These were days of bluest skies, trees filled with wind, wonderful wildness, wheels and movement. We thought we might fly and perhaps we did. We were all things and most ourselves then. No room could hold us and no time could contain us."
—*Sandra Ortiz Taylor*

RIVER PEOPLE: AN INVOCATION

I dream a village
spread along the river banks
where my grandmother's house is now.
Smoke from the fires blows and invokes this vision
of people, of makers baking rounded pots—
this pot, etched with the groove
from the ridged fingernail
of the *mama grande*
de mi mama grande.

These are my people, the river people,
whose language sounds like water moving lucid
over river stones,
round and moving stones,
the knocking of one into the next,
of my wisdom striking yours.

Book One

EQUINOX

My mother sits at the long table in her mother's kitchen, a taco between her thumb and middle finger. She has felt a twinge. It is 1939. Over her head the sun, Venus, and Mercury have all conjoined in Libra. Perhaps she has not felt a twinge, after all.

She sets the taco down. Her mother looks at her from the head of the table. Her father, a second-generation German, eats his taco while my father lectures him patiently on Rosicrucianism. Across the table sits my Aunt Pearl, who wears her hair in silver sausages. She is the same age as my grandmother and is married to my Uncle Arthur, who is twenty years her junior and who adores her, calling her Baby and enduring her five Chihuahuas with their bulging eyes and savage temperaments. Uncle Arthur sits next to Pearl, spooning refried beans onto a huge flour tortilla and nodding whenever Baby pauses for breath.

My mother feels it again. She feels the moon slip into Aquarius. My grandmother rises to her feet, sits down. Passes the basket of tortillas to her son.

Two hours later my mother, her long hair plaited down her back, is propped up in bed smoking a cigarette in the Queen of the Angels hospital while her mother knits at her feet. Her mother is a stolid, dark wedge. The sound from her knitting needles is slight but steady. Against the sound of the needles the pain takes shape, bulging and shifting like a determined serpent. She stubs out her Camel, raises her knees, sees herself as a child, lying in a basket on the porch of a farmhouse in the Imperial Valley. Book One

3

Her mother moves close, lays a brown hand on her ankle. She does not like hospitals. Doctors make people sick. Her own thirteen children were born in her bed in her house by the river. Río de Los Angeles. She lays her hand now on her child to ease the pain. Her youngest daughter. Her Juanita.

A nun comes in. There is a faint aroma of Clorox and starch. My mother mistakes her for an angel because she is so beautifully laundered. All in white, with a black rosary at her waist. "It is time," she says, removing a hypodermic from the folded white towel. My grandmother moves to the window.

"What's that?" asks my mother.

"You had this before," says the nun. "It's on your chart. The doctor wants you to have it."

My grandmother studies the moon. Fifth house. Mars in Aquarius is good, she thinks.

"Twilight Sleep," says the nun. "When you awake you will remember nothing." Her sudden movement forward, with the needle, the sudden swaying of her hips sets in motion the rosary. The last thing my mother hears is the almost imperceptible click of the beads, of her mother's knitting needles.

In this picture my sister is sitting in a tiny Mexican chair holding me in her lap. She is wearing some kind of peasant costume: a soft white cap on her head, sculpting her dark brow like a fringe of flower petals, a flowered cotton dress, covered by a starched, white apron. Her small feet are wedged for support into the rungs of the chair. I am naked, and so new that my legs have not quite unfolded. Her brown arms encircle me. She smiles at the camera.

My father holds the Kodak. **PHOTOGRAPH 1**

It has accordioned out toward my sister and me. My mother leans, one hand on her hip, next to my father. They stand on the patio of the new house my father designed with the Los Angeles architect who abruptly left the state and possibly the country owing more money than he could ever repay. Every hinge and doorknob in the house is a replica taken from Mexican houses. The white plaster house curled about the patio has thirteen doors, all opening onto this patio. On the windows are authentic *rejas*, hand forged in Olvera Street, to keep out bandits. There are hand-painted Mexican tiles in the bathrooms and red tiles on the floors. The handsome house perches at the apex of five costly lots in Silver Lake on a curving gravel road known locally as the horseshoe.

The tiny baby, drooling in her sister's lap has occasioned all this expense. The other three people had lived happily in the small rented house on Sixty-fifth Street, until the Christmas night my mother still commemorates in perfume. Life changed for the three people, two of whom had always believed there would never be more than three in the family.

MIRRORS

I was conceived on Christmas night 1938. How do I know this? Arithmetically I know this because I was born exactly and precisely nine months later, on September twenty-fifth. Poetically I know this because of a beautiful blue bottle my mother always kept on her glass perfume tray.

Glass perfume trays provide exercises in perception, doubling their contents like placid lakes throwing back trees and deer to hidden observers. And I *was* an observer. Whenever my mother went into the side yard to hang laundry I would sneak into her dressing room, part of the adult compound, a territory always strangely mysterious to my sister and me. There was something forbidden, something invisible but pervasive as a lingering fragrance.

The door to the heart of this off-limits world was my mother's dressing room, a sanctuary guarded appropriately enough by a mirrored door. From the doorknob radiated a single crack crossing the width of the door like the faultline traversing the California coast. Or like a strand of barbed wire.

I stand before the door, studying myself. I am small and fair. My face looks angelic—despite my mission—and I am wearing overalls of stout corduroy, graced on the bib with a Quixotic windmill. I wipe my palm down the side of my trousers, then twist the porcelain knob, and the door swings open easily.

Inside smells like my mother. Before me stands a mirrored dressing table neatly laid out. I approach in reverence. Experimentally I lift the lid on her powder box. The box is covered with eyes and there is a whooshing sound as carefully I expose the delicate powder. Part of my mother's smell is inside. Woman smell. I stick my finger into the softness, then remember my mother outside, hanging clothes.

Quickly I glance over at her shoes arranged in neat rows, cherry red shoe trees bulging out the open toes. I long to touch the shoe trees and bend them out of the shoes, slip my small feet inside a pair of spectator pumps and go clacking down the hall, but there is not time for that, there will never be time for that. Instead I look at what I came for, the blue bottle.

Blue prism, clear and dark, luminous but obscure, a glowing kind of blue, blue as a lake this cool blue glass in my hand, the blue way my mother smells when she disappears into her beauty leaving my sister and me and my father on the outside, alone together in the blue fragrance of a recollection.

With the glass stopper I anoint each pulse. In the mirror a cherubic face looks back, the inverted Christ child.

I hear the kitchen door slam and jam the stopper back, and like a jewel thief set my mother's Christmas Night carefully back in its place on the tray.

SHOE TREES

Those are my father's shoes. Sixteen pair. They sit expectant in three tiered rows, like fans on bleachers, before the game begins.

My father's closet, like the rest of the house, he has designed himself. The closet, like the rest of the house, is designed so that every human need can be met, preferably before it is experienced.

There is a certain futility about this plan.

I am thinking now of the little electrical device coming out of the Mexican tile floor in our dining room. This little mechanism rests near my father's right foot, where he sits in the only chair with arms, at the dining room table. This machine is designed to summon the maid, should more butter be required. In my life we never had a maid.

My father is a great projector. The heart of a projector is often a little large and often particularly sensitive to the rigors of reality. But this one is good for another dozen years or so. In the meantime his mind busily sketches out plans, some of which he will realize.

The closet testifies to this fact. Not only does his closet hold his sixteen pair of shoes running from his black and white wing tips on the upper left level to his topsiders on the lower right, but this closet has built-in drawers that slide out easily, if one fits a small hand into the scooped-out handle.

This one, for example, holds his socks, neatly tucked into burrito-shaped bundles that may be easily turned inside out, always revealing impeccably maintained sock mates.

My father, of course, does not maintain these burritos. It is 1942 and my mother maintains these socks, as well as those belonging to me and my sister, as well as the nylon hose burritos she tucks into silken pockets hanging inside her own closet door.

Socks fill my father's entire drawer, beginning on the left with his dress stockings, which must be supported by a fascinating garter system on each of his well-turned legs, and ending with his cotton socks that go with the Sperry topsiders.

There are no shirts in this ample drawer, for my father will not have his shirts folded. No. My mother irons these shirts and places them on hangers, all facing the same way, in the part of the closet designed to hold dress shirts.

Another drawer holds my father's underwear, boxer shorts of discreet shade and cut. These must be ironed too, as well as the stacks of giant handkerchiefs nestled next to the shorts.

I once bolted unexpectedly into my parents' bedroom and caught my father standing cranelike, one socked foot balancing on the hardwood floor, the other searching for the entrance to one of these selfsame pair of boxer shorts.

The drawer slides in easily. I use the cutout handle as a toe rest, and pull myself up to see the desklike top of the built-in cabinet. His sonorous change rests here when he is at home, but today he is at the recording studio with the Gordon Jenkins Orchestra taping the music for "Our Miss Brooks," and my mother has stepped out for just a minute to have coffee with Catherine, two doors down the horseshoe.

Next to where the change goes are various implements of measurement: a stop watch, a pocket watch, a sextant in a black box with a lid, and a compass in a mahogany box without a lid. On clear nights my father takes my sister and me out onto the patio to shoot the stars. He looks into his sextant and speaks of latitude and longitude. We look for bears and swords and dancing women in the skies. We must learn navigation, he tells us. One day we will all sail around the world together in a great boat. Using this very sextant. I touch the lid, do not lift it off.

Behind the watch, compass, sextant there is a springed mechanism holding ties that accordions out from the wall. I finger them. They will whistle through my father's fingers as he knots them carefully, studying himself in the mirror mounted on the closet door.

This is how, he will say, standing behind me, guiding my hands in the tying of the huge knot. Like this.

I guide the tie rack carefully into place and lower myself. The shoes are last. I count them. There is one empty place on the far rack, gaping like a missing tooth. The brown wing tips are gone. I see my father, beckoned by the baton of Gordon Jenkins, rise onto his brown wing tips and deliver a clarinet solo.

Leaning deep into the closet, resting my right hand on the middle level, I pick up one brown and white saddle oxford by the bulb of the shoe tree, then the other. The shoe trees look like wooden feet and flex and bend as I ease them out. My own feet float now in magic shoes laced tight. I clunk forth toward my mother's mirror.

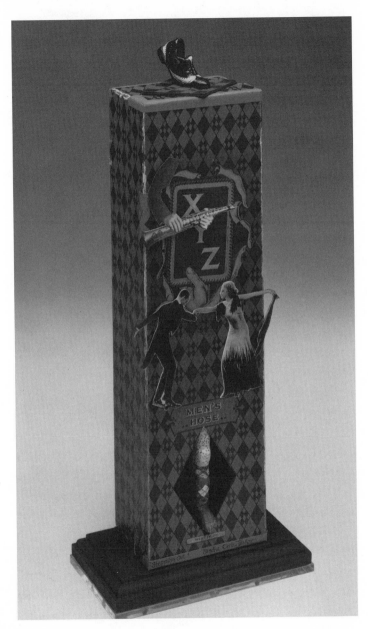

Stepping Out. Front.

POLAR PALACE

Before these shoes all came to rest in the closets lovingly designed by my father, my parents had to meet and find one another indispensable, in myriad ways, to their continued existence. This happened in 1933 at the indoor ice skating rink on Melrose Avenue.

They are lacing on their skates, perfect strangers.

They are balancing on scarred wooden benches at opposite ends of the refreshment stand, lacing up rented skates. On the backs of their skates large, hand-drawn numbers reveal their shoe sizes to the world. Organ music plays over the loud speaker; steam rises from the ice.

My mother has arrived with her three sisters: Bertha, Thelma, and Ella. They are smoking cigarettes self-consciously, tugging at their long laces, and pretending not to know their two brothers who have been sent along to keep an eye on them, though at a distance.

The brothers' eyes are not on their sisters at all. My Uncle David's eyes have fallen on a raven-haired beauty in a leather jacket, whose escort is a burly member of a motorcycle gang called the Thirteen Black Cats. Uncle David's left eye will, in due course, be blackened by this gentleman, but not on this particular Sunday.

My other uncle, Uke the Duke, equally unerring, has singled out for his appreciation my father's present wife, Doreen. My father bends over his black figure skates, shaping the loops of the laces into double knots, and fails to see my uncle eyeing his wife.

He sits up now, keen to Doreen's body language, and follows her gaze to that of Uke the Duke, who now bends his own head to his skates in apparent innocence.

Nobody is even on the ice yet.

My father inclines his head to Doreen, rises, and walks expertly on blades to the refreshment counter for coffee. He glances again at Uke the Duke, whose face seems to him scoured out during the glacial period. He marks my uncle's ornate, silver belt buckle, his cowboy shirt with the morning glories winding up his arms; watches him get up and hobble over to a woman of matchless beauty, a woman with long dark hair done up in a cunning way behind, a woman with eyes like the sounding board of a guitar. Juanita.

His heart suddenly strums. He hears her laugh, a husky woman laugh; a wise laugh, though she is young. Too young. Next to her is a second woman, perhaps her sister, with the same features—the dark eyes, high cheekbones, abundant hair twisted into a bun, aquiline nose—but all slightly awry, a little discordant in a way that sets off, heightens the beauty of her sister. Next to this second woman are two more, one impossibly fat, the other impossibly thin. My father sips his coffee while the cup intended for his wife cools at his left elbow.

A voice comes over the loudspeaker welcoming everybody to the Polar Palace. "All skate," it says, "all skate slowly please."

The next time they come skating, my father has left Doreen at home and my mother has pulled up in front of the Polar Palace on the back of a Harley Davidson. She slips out of her date's black leather jacket and unbinds her hair from a silk scarf covered with roses that her sister has loaned her, the sister who is now walking down the center isle of Grauman's Chinese Theater wearing red silk pajamas and carrying a flashlight that guides William Holden safely to his seat. My mother hands the jacket to the youth who one week ago blackened the left eye of her brother David and knots the scarf around her neck.

She plans to put her hair up in the rest room, but before she can accomplish that purpose, she rounds a corner and bumps into my father. Hair falls all around them, shimmering. My father has a quick vision of the perfect luxury of hair, of being wound in a nest of hair, a passion of hair, he feels it brush across his face in a way he can never forget and never express.

But he is already married. My mother points this out.

Two weeks later my mother is skating, hands crossed, with her impossibly thin sister Bertha. The organ plays something romantic. My mother closes her eyes for just an instant and thinks of the attorney who looks like Clark Gable and wears beautiful clothes, beautiful shoes. Plays the saxophone on radio. When she reaches the dangerous turn, she must open her eyes.

She hears him behind her, the slight scrape scrape of metal on ice; feels him taking her free elbow. His teeth are perfect, she thinks.

But she is not anybody's fool. She tells him this.

No, he says. You don't understand.

She feels her ankles start to give, collapse in. A way she does not like to skate. She looks at this man, this musical attorney. His cheeks are pink, like tiny steaks. He says he is getting a divorce. Her sister lets go her hand.

Stepping Out. Back.

On a plaid blanket in Mrs. Bancarrol's backyard sit two cherubic children, about two years old, perhaps less. Their heads are covered in blond curls and they both wear corduroy trousers and T-shirts. They smile into Mr. Bancarrol's camera, squinting their blue eyes with pleasure. These charming babes may perhaps be the Bancarrols' twin sons. On the other hand, they could as easily be the Bancarrols' twin daughters. Actually they are neither.

PHOTOGRAPH 2

Mrs. Bancarrol and my mother became pregnant at precisely the same moment, living—as they did—three houses away from each other, though each with a different husband and a different cast of mind altogether. Perhaps bearing a child was not even on Mrs. Bancarrol's mind on Christmas night 1938. For she was English and lived with her English lord in a house resembling Anne Hathaway's cottage three houses away from the Taylor hacienda. Instead of children they had three airedales, whom they took riding every afternoon, with all the windows rolled down, and the dogs sitting back in unconcealed pleasure, their tongues lolling out, and festive scarves tied around their curly heads to ward off the earache. All this could only have happened in Southern California.

Not only were Mrs. Bancarrol and my mother, the English lady and the Indian maiden, both pregnant at the same time but they had selected the same names for their respective children: Brian if it was a boy, Sheila if a girl. Mrs. Bancarrol planned to have the girl and my mother intended to have the boy.

Here I should discuss my family philosophy on my mother's side, the Ortiz y Cabares philosophy. The beauty of it is that it neither presupposes a concerned deity nor denies one; it is perhaps Catholic. My grandmother said, "Que será será" and my mother said, "What will be will be." This philosophy would be difficult to refute.

Therefore, the boy was born to the Bancarrols and the girl to the Taylors. In any event there was no difficulty about names, their having been interchangeable from the first, though the four parents gazing idly at this selfsame photograph might have wondered a little at these identical, androgynous children, until they remembered Brian and I were delivered at different hospitals, his Anglican and mine Catholic, notwithstanding the pope's view on second marriages.

To the photograph of Brian and me sitting on the blanket, there is a companion photograph. This second photograph is identical to the first, except that between Brian and me has been inserted a third child, this one larger, though perhaps a little younger. The curls on Brian and me are coiled tight, rather like the curls on his mother's airedales, while those on the third child hang down in sausages, with a fat ribbon wrapped around them and tied on top the head. This is Becky.

Now that I look more closely I see that there is, after all, a difference in our expressions in the second photograph. Brian's innocence has taken on a hint of fear whereas mine has taken on a touch of roguishness. Becky is activating the paradox of our twin identities. Becky is dedicating her young life to terrorizing Brian, as the picture is being snapped.

It is a typical day six or seven years later. We have been playing at Becky's house. I like to play at Becky's house because it is so American and because her mother, Catherine, is seldom home. Today is no exception and Becky and I have therefore already called the drugstore on the phone to ask if they have Prince Albert in a can, called Information to ask the operator if she knew where Catherine hid her Mrs. See's candy, and eaten several dog biscuits apiece. We are lying on Becky's bed now, a four poster with a Steven Foster bedspread that says Old Folks at Home all over it, accompanied by depictions of black people in subservient positions. The same pictures and captions run up and down the walls. My eyes are closed because Americana tends to make me dizzy.

Becky is thinking. Suddenly she sits up, evil glinting in her green eyes. When Becky gets this look in her eye and her mother is home, she gets a beating. In fact the venetian blinds have slats missing all up and down them where Catherine has seized an implement of correction, hoping to avert the disaster these green eyes may eventually bring down on them all. But Catherine is at a meeting of the steering committee for the Salvation Army and so her daughter sits up and says, with perfect equanimity, "Let's go torment Brian."

She always puts it this way: "Let's go torment Brian." Catherine must have initially suggested the vocabulary, perhaps in a previous frenzy of punishment, but we have all adopted it or at least understand its meaning.

Becky jams three or four dog biscuits into her jeans and we march on Brian. Since Becky's white-frame house with the green shutters is on the lower level of the gravel road forming the horseshoe, Brian can see us coming from the upper window of Anne Hathaway's cottage, where he has been lying in bed reading *The Wind in the Willows*. Becky pounds at the cottage door.

When Mrs. Bancarrol opens the little window in the door, Becky subdues her eyes and asks, "Can Brian play?" Mrs. Bancarrol looks at me. Imperceptibly I shake my head.

"Brian's reading, luv," she says. "Thanks anyway." She swings closed the little window.

We walk back down the hill, munching the dog biscuits. My sister is lubing her Radio Flyer in the driveway. It's upside down and she's clicking our mother's sewing machine oil onto all moving parts.

"Brian can't play," says Becky ruefully.

My sister understands the full significance of this statement and suggests instead we play war. The script for war is as predictable as the soap operas my family is all in the habit of listening to. My sister and I are radio babies and are learning our art, each in her way, by grasping the essential principle of repetition.

The script of war has to do not so much with the central violent act but with the responsive healing. My sister, a downed pilot, has a serious injury that requires the undivided attention of a nurse. A secondary element of the plot is that the injured pilot must be transported from the field into the remote temporary hospital.

The casting for this psychodrama is as unwavering as the plot. My sister always plays the downed pilot, Becky always plays the nurse, and I always play the horse who pulls the wagon conveying the downed pilot. We are untroubled by the anachronistic juxtaposition of fighter plane and horse-drawn wagon. Becky hates being the nurse, but I don't mind being the horse. The role has an appealing simplicity.

Becky has run off to get her nurse's hat, my sister has gone into the house to find her medals, and I stand and wait with horselike fidelity, having really no costuming requirements at all.

I put out my arms into the afternoon silence and turn slowly, slowly in the California sunshine, and am turning still when Mrs. Bancarrol drives by, over crackling gravel, waving, Brian and the airedales grinning from the back seat.

DINNER 1942

We are wearing our pajamas with the feet in them, my sister and I. We are bathed and rosy, playing in the living room before dinner. We sit on a large rug woven through with images of the Corn Goddess. Behind the rug is an authentic replica of a Mexican hearth, though to us it looks like an igloo, and when it is swept clean we sometimes crouch in it, pretending to eat raw fish. But it is winter in California and the fireplace has been in recent use, though not on this particular late afternoon. We have assembled on the rug a collection of Indian dolls and woven baskets that contribute to the room's decor.

I hold their soft bodies in my hands, study their intricate belts, the beads around their necks, their tiny earrings. My sister is trying to remove the clothes from a brave. She is exhibiting an early scientific interest, one which only recently led to her inserting five hundred straight pins through the hole in the rosy ceramic lips of her doll Anne.

In fact Anne was herself a scientific experiment. My father promised my sister a doll with the world's first toy digestive system, accompanied by a steamer trunk of clothes—to scale—if she would stop biting her nails. My sister stopped biting her nails until Anne was hers, then she resumed. My sister's logical mind will prove a frustration to my father on more than one occasion.

My sister is carefully peeling back the trousers of the Indian brave. Then a chime sounds.

These chimes are part of an electronic network my father has designed into the house. Like the foot buzzer under the dining room table intended to call the maid, these little doorbell like devices, when pushed, convey an obscure message to every room in the house. My mother must mean: Come to the dining room and eat your dinner.

Because of the peculiar floor plan conceived by my father, this buzzer system might almost seem necessary. The living room is separate from the rest of the house and can only be reached by going outside and traversing a veranda. This arrangement, like so many others having to do with our household, is strange, but my sister and I will not begin to comprehend just how strange for four or five decades.

My sister pulls up the brave's pants and we return the family of Indians to their various stations in niches built into the Mexican igloo. Then we go outside, cross the veranda, and enter through the dining room door.

The long, dark table is set for two. We sit down, and Mother puts our plates on place mats before us, as if we are customers in a diner. Baked potatoes steam and melt their pats of butter, fresh spinach nuzzles a lamb chop. We eat, drink milk, leaving white moustaches on our upper lips, laugh.

Mother is in the kitchen cooking a second dinner: the grown-up dinner. The second dinner will share some items from the earlier menu, but will be more varied, more exotic. There will be a table cloth, wine, candles. Perhaps music.

By the time we are in bed it is still starkest daylight outside. Though Mother has said the days are getting shorter, somehow it feels they are getting longer. We can read comic books but not get up.

Finally we hear Daddy come home. He walks into the room, tall above our beds, bends to kiss us, his whiskers scratchy but scented still. Growing smaller, he pulls the door to, behind him. From the dining room we hear the distant music of crystal and silver, ghostlike conversation on the dimming air.

AFTERLIFE

My sister and I are in the yellow bathtub, bubbles up to our chests, playing laundry. We soap up three or four washcloths and stick them against the sides of the tub. Then we run the back brush over them like a mangle iron, fold them in fours, and stack them. As we perfect our technique, we invent disasters. The soaped washcloths unstick from the tub side and slide back down into the bubbly waters. We groan in dismay, begin the process again.

My father is in the next room, dressed for the evening, practicing his clarinet. He has on black shoes with creamy tops that look like iced cookies. He wets his lips and places the reed on his lower lip. Sound scales up and down the walls; our washcloths slide into the bubbly water. Mother comes in wearing a pale pink slip and earrings. She hums under her breath "My funny valentine, sweet comic valentine." There is a hint of Christmas Night on the air. They are going out. They will have dinner in Hollywood at Nicks Seafood Grotto and bring us home bags of crab claws that we will have for breakfast, only not where Daddy can see us. Anything that is not bacon and eggs will have to be eaten outside under the eucalyptus tree. Enchiladas are like that.

My mother lets a warm drop of water fall into her Maybelline mascara and blends it carefully with her tiny brush. Then she leans forward into the triple mirror, the brush poised.

At that very moment, in the bathroom window suddenly appears the face of the baby-sitter, Margie. "Hi, it's me," she says.

My mother gives a little controlled lurch, steadies herself, then says, lowering the brush, "Come on in."

When Margie gets to the door, she thunders on it with her fist. The clarinet stops. Mother towels us off, puts my pajamas on me. My sister does her own.

In the dining room Margie and my father are talking about God. My father does not believe in God; Margie does. They are both interested in God. My father will talk about God with anybody. He invites in Jehovah's Witnesses and talks to them until they turn pale.

We sit down before steaming bowls of Hormel's chili con carne with fresh chopped onions, plates of tortillas with melted jack cheese.

My father is called Jack. He leans forward, the clarinet balanced upright on his right knee. Margie, always large, grows larger when she speaks of the afterlife. Her face loses definition, looks like un-baked bread. My father tells her there is no life after death. My mother comes in, stuffing little objects into a red beaded bag. Her face is defined and beautiful. My mother never speaks of God. In-stead she asks Margie how her boyfriend is. Margie brightens, tells them about their date watching the news headlines flashing on the Times building downtown. My father pulls his clarinet into three pieces, then they leave.

I look at the crescent of cool tortilla lying on my plate. It is about to begin. We ask Margie to tell us about heaven.

Margie knows heaven in great detail. She knows heaven the way an employee of the public works department would know heaven: by its streets, sidewalks, gutters. These streets, sidewalks, gutters are made entirely of fourteen-carat gold. In my mind I see a steam roller cruising along, crushing gold into shapely roads. Light refracts in all directions. I see a splendid glittering world with no one in it.

We never ask about the missing people. And in fact Margie's own detailed view of the afterlife may include people, angels, God. But as small daughters of an atheist, we admit the streets paved with gold but instinctively deny the inhabitants. We see the afterlife as a celestial ghost town.

Avoiding the issue of inhabitants, we question Margie intently, as if we are lawyers. Partly we are curious and partly we are trying to delay for as long as possible the second, inevitable half of the evening.

We know that her attention span is not as long as our own. We know her mood will suddenly careen, that we will have done something bad, something requiring punishment. Tonight she is describing the rubies and emeralds around the street drains in heaven when suddenly a look travels from one of her eyes to the next as if she is spelling out the messages on the Times building.

"You children are bad," she says. "I'm going home. I'm leaving you."

She sets us up on the kitchen counter, one of us on either side of the double sink. "I'm leaving you now," she says, her voice gaining volume as if she is an actor at the Greek Theater or something, shouting from a distance through a mask. "I'm going home."

We hear her moving through the house, her heavy feet echoing back her position like radar in a submarine movie. We listen to distant clicks of lights going out while we sit high on the counter in the florescent kitchen, the room she will visit last.

"I'm really leaving now," she says, smiling crookedly, lawlessly, her white sausage of a finger poised over the switch.

"Please don't go." At last we say it.

"You've been bad." The light goes out. Heavy feet move toward the door. The door swings open, then shut. We listen, don't move.

"She's not really going," whispers my sister. "She's standing there right now."

We hear the feet move off across the veranda, hear them take the three steps, giant feet in the dark. Then the heavy outer door creaks open, the one the family never uses, the iron ring clanking under her hand. Then the door bangs shut.

We sit high in the silence and darkness waiting. Pale light from the moon streams in the kitchen window, turning the kitchen floor into a street of gold. In a while she will come back, laughing, worried we'll tell our parents.

But what if this time she doesn't? My breath comes in suddenly, like a sob.

"You know she's standing out there," says my sister, leaning forward over the edge of the counter, measuring the distance to the floor, calculating the time until she will be able to leap down, turn, hold her arms up for me.

RED CAR

The Red Car is coming. My mother and I stand on the hill beneath my father's house and watch the electric train approach across an expansion bridge that looks like the kind I see in Flash Gordon movies at the Dirty Dime Theater, the kind where trains start falling off cliffs and then it says "Continued Next Week" and we have to wait until next Saturday to see what will happen.

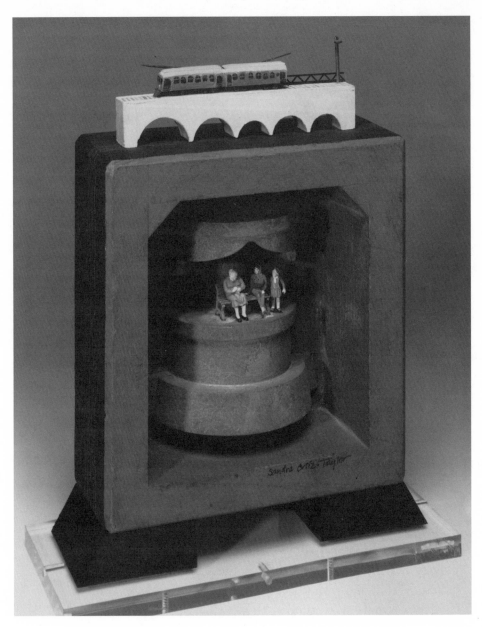

Waiting for the Red Car

What happens today is the dentist. My teeth are fine. It is my mother's teeth again. She pulls at her white gloves, takes my hand in hers. Sparks fly off the wires overhead and shoot out of the wheels. There is the smell of hot metal, and then the rubbery unfolding of doors.

The street car smells like dimes. We hold tight while the Red Car picks up speed. My mother hands me two tokens and I drop them into the little glass tower and watch them fall from level to level, flashing like silver fish until they disappear into the bottom. We weave down the aisle, looking for two places together.

We sit down on green velvet seats with a pattern like zebras. The conductor leans forward and flips a lever that makes the glass tower eat the tokens and coins. He sits very straight, bouncing in round waves on his soft seat as we rocket toward town on the Red Car.

But first comes the tunnel. We race toward it, the car half filled by now, the glass tower working fast on those tokens; bright tickets and crinkly transfers stick out of silver clips on the backs of zebra seats, my nose presses slippery against the cool window. First comes the breath of cave air and hot grease, then the windows blink from bright into dark, lights overhead come on, then the rocking of zebra velvet and the sucking sound as we pass, clicking and rocking into the heart of downtown.

The doors fold open onto an underground world. Behind us the conductor slings the seats around—racheta racheta—so they face back where we came from. As if slung, we shoot out, make our way quickly past old men leaning against the wall, others curled up on beds of newspaper, past newspaper boys and old ladies selling flowers.

Outside smells like sun and popcorn. We stand blinking. This is MacArthur Park. My mother pulls me past the man talking about

God, the one my father likes to hear. Geese crowd around an old lady with a shopping cart of rusty lettuce. She opens her mouth wide to call them. Her teeth are dark and crooked.

My mother has noticed—I can tell—noticed the teeth because to her teeth are maybe the most important thing. She gets that look. I know she is running her tongue up over her own teeth, checking for something.

Next thing I know we are in the tall building that smells like medicine and cigarettes. My mother signs the dentist's register, starts reading a *Vogue,* very fast. Together we ignore the clattering scream of the drill coming through the wall. I close my eyes and think of us rocketing back in the Red Car.

My father says it is a shame about my mother's teeth: a woman that beautiful. He tells us to think about my grandmother and how she had thirteen children, all needing this and that so no dentist for my mother. Now her teeth are filled with blue silver.

In a minute she will go in to the dentist and sit in his green chair where he will tilt her back until her mouth falls open. I will sit here by myself, next to this window, and read the small books placed here for children.

HUNTING SCENE

My grandmother is plucking her chin whiskers, my Texas grandmother. Her vast chin appears in the magnifying side of her looking glass. I am lying on her chenille bedspread and watching this ritual with great scientific interest.

Her room is called the maid's room, having been designed by

my father to house the maid we will never have. Yet it will always be called the maid's room, even when my sister and I inherit it in our turn. The title of this room for us comes to signify a place far from the prying ears of parents, a place where convention can be turned upside down.

Hence my lawless lolling on my grandmother's bed and her open invitation to share her most private secrets.

She gives her chin one last search-and-destroy investigation, then hands the mirror to me. On one side of the mirror my blue eyes appear in the face I have come to think of as mine. I turn the mirror over and my features grow, distort, swim at me. I search blond chin fuzz for black whiskers. Then carefully I fold the mirror into its lovely red casing with the English hunting scene frozen on it. Two men on brown horses turn in their saddles as if watching a beautiful woman who does not quite appear in the scene. They wear red coats. Behind them a sea of dogs glitters.

My grandmother is stepping into her flesh-colored drawers, my grandmother who rode a horse and went to Baylor University. She steadies herself with her right hand and pulls with the left. Her hands are thin and covered with skin you can see through. Looking into my grandmother's hands is like looking into the fishpond of our next door neighbors. On the surface is a glitter, and just beneath you can see dark shapes moving. My grandmother does not mind if very gently my sister and I press together the skin on her hands, shaping it into ridges that when released gradually fade back into the surface of a pond.

I crawl across her bed and open the drawer in her bedside stand carefully. Next to the black leather bible I place the mirror, take a quick survey—letters tied with a pink ribbon, old and curling like treasure maps, a pin cushion like a tomato, her silver thimble (enormous on my thumb)—then slip the mirror carefully into its drawer and close it. Her teeth float undisturbed in a glass by her bed.

My grandmother nods when I look at her. Slowly I pick up the glass of teeth—glittering with California sun—and carry it into the bathroom, while she puts on her seersucker house dress. The teeth seem enormous and have bubble-gum tinted gums. Horse teeth look like these.

She fishes them out with her long Texas fingers and brushes them vigorously with a toothbrush and Kolynose toothpaste. I sit on the toilet lid, watching. She wedges the top teeth in, accompanied by a little sound of air as the plastic sucks onto the cave of her mouth. When she joins the bottoms on, she makes little kissing sounds that settle the teeth in for the day. Now, when she speaks she will whistle.

The Fuller Brush Man hair brush arranges her gray and wisping locks against her long face, making the deep-set dark eyes sink farther in. She turns glittering eyes on me. She is ready.

But for what?

We hear a cupboard bang in the kitchen. My grandmother is listening to the morning sounds of the woman in whose house she lives.

From the way she stands I think of the hunting scene on her mirror and of the watching people, the quivering animals. "Tell me about your pony," I say. "Tell me a story."

She moves to the window, slowly, her hip remembering now its break last Easter, lowers herself into the skirted chair, remembering, perhaps. Remembering her dead husband, my father's father, seeing him standing at night on the roof of his saddle shop in Beaumont, his telescope trained on the heavens.

She takes in a sharp breath. "He was a chestnut," she says, "and he was mine." The "was" whistles between us. She looks out the window, sees the hibiscus bending in morning breeze.

"You rode him at night," I prompt.

"No, never at night.

"You raced the train," I say. "You went to college."

"Yes," she says, leaning forward slightly in her chair. "Baylor University. This was a long time ago, before you were born. In those days, you see, young ladies were not expected to go to college. I remember one night I said to my papa—that'd be your great grandaddy—'Papa, what would you say if . . .'"

My grandmother's imagination is at last taking the hurdles: through the window, over the white stucco wall my father has built out of milk cartons and cement, over the hedge, past the clothesline, into the dry and blowing fields, while I sit listening to the soft sibilant sounds of my grandmother's false teeth.

SINGER

My mother and father do not sleep in the same bed. Being Southern Californians they sleep in Hollywood beds but they are pushed very close. When my mother makes the beds every morning, she swings a triangle between them so she can tuck the sheets in tight. Then she swings them back.

My mother is bent over my father's bed with great concentration. She is pinning gossamer sheets of paper to fabric and cutting around them with her pinking sheers. Sometimes she pauses and makes a quick line with tailor's chalk. Three pins protrude from between her lips, and I must not speak to her. She is creating.

I watch her from the window seat in the ancestral bedroom. I have a cold and have been tucked in here with pillow and comforter and books. It is winter, a sunny morning bright as tin, and the eucalyptus are tossing their heads sportively outside my window.

My mother has a red hibiscus tucked into the bun of hair coiled up on her head. She is wearing a red house dress, freshly laundered and ironed, covered in a pattern of pale yellow sombreros. Her lips are red, too, Revlon Fire and Ice, lips that grip their cargo of pins; fingernails red, too, as they emerge through the finger holes of her pinking shears; also her red richly lacquered toenails, emerging through yellow open-toed wedgies. Red is my favorite color.

My mother became an artist when she quit Belmont High School in the tenth grade and went to work in the yo-yo factory. I see her bend over her first yo-yo: a deep plum color. She dips her brush into burnt sienna, then with a few deft strokes gives birth to an iris, into which—like a skillful bee—she installs the pistil and stamen. My mother, had she not met my father at the Polar Palace Ice Skating Rink, might have become Georgia O'Keeffe.

After the yo-yo factory she was hired in a shop, trimming hats. Sophisticated hats, hats worthy of Greta Garbo, hats of subtle curve and raffish feather. Hats of such delicacy and design that the owner of the hat shop was overcome with love, while his wife was overcome with jealousy. This was a domestic problem that could be resolved only by firing my mother.

Artists are not necessarily appreciated in their time. My mother bends now, picking up the side panel of a dress and holding it up to the light. She is exacting. She has the entire dress assembled in her mind, and holds up the pieces to see how they will ultimately conform themselves to the vision. Measure, balance, line, color, pattern. She runs a tape measure across the collar. Shakes her head. Trims with her massive scissors, forsaking the lines here, knowing better than the lines, after all. By making her own dresses, suits, coats even, she knows she will not—as other women must—see herself coming and going. She smiles at the thought of never seeing herself coming and going.

She is ready for the machine. The Singer. From the side drawer filled with spools of thread she selects five or six, holds each one against the fabric until the ideal one identifies itself. The others she slips back onto their tiny dowels. Now she must make a bobbin. She seats herself on the bench, back erect, like a concert pianist. Clicking noises emanate; cogs and levers disengaged, reengaged. My mother's hand rises to the silver wheel; she gives it just the slightest encouraging spin, beginning at the precise instant the pumping action with her feet. For a moment it seems organ music will emanate. Instead, the bobbin begins to fill itself with pale pink thread, weaving back and forth under the rhythmic exertions of my mother's expert feet. Then she removes the bobbin and bites the thread in two.

Whenever she does this in my father's presence he shudders with an apprehension of the frail nature of beauty and the transiency of human life, not to mention the high cost of dentists, particularly hers. But he is downtown at the recording studio practicing for tomorrow night's "Our Miss Brooks" show, while my mother, high on a hill overlooking Silver Lake, practices her art.

The clicking noises now repeat themselves backwards, and my mother prepares to thread the machine. This must be done quickly and in the correct sequence. My mother places the pink spool on its spindle, then zigs and zags the thread's end through the tiny arms and eyes and levers until she arrives at the needle. Next she applies the thread to her mouth, shapes it to a point between her index finger and thumb, and plunges. Damn, she says. She turns on the floor lamp next to the machine, rolls the thread end again, and voilà! Now she snaps in the bobbin from underneath, turns the wheel once by hand, dredges up the bobbin thread, and is ready to begin.

She pauses for a cigarette, standing on the patio just outside the bedroom door, still in sight, her foot upraised, resting on the low wall. She has begun to hum. Sewing is accompanied by humming, singing, and whistling. Humming when she has cigarettes or straight pins in her mouth, singing and whistling if not.

My mother can plunge two fingers in her mouth, and whistle across three hills for my sister and me.

She reseats herself at the bench. Up goes the pressure foot, then down onto the fabric. My mother's hand rises to the wheel, gives a spin, her feet begin: "Someone's rocking my dreamboat," she sings, feeding the cloth, shaping the dress.

At noon she brings me Campbell's chicken noodle soup on a tray and two flour tortillas, warmed with butter. A glass of milk. She never eats when she's sewing. She has a cigarette and a cup of black coffee, her chair pulled up to the window seat.

"Did you learn to sew in school?" I ask her.

My mother stares at me because she does not believe anybody ever learned anything of value in school. Like all her brothers and sisters, she left in tenth grade. "I just knew," she says, blowing a puff of smoke in the direction of her sewing teacher. "*She* didn't like it. Miss Hanks. She said I did everything backwards. Kept making me rip out seams. She wanted me to do it *her* way."

"What did you tell her?"

"I told her she only slowed me down."

"And . . . ?" I said, biting into a tortilla.

"She said she'd fail me."

"Did she?"

"How could she? I sewed better than she did. She did give me a D though." She laughs, low and reckless, sends another cloud of smoke in the direction of Miss Hanks's shade, then gathers up my dishes.

"Will I like school?" I ask her.

"Some people like it," she says, heading for the kitchen, the tray aloft.

There is something generous in this statement, a generosity in the way she lifts the tray, in the way she may have forgiven Miss Hanks.

Because it is a long way to the other bathroom, I decide to use this one: theirs. It is yellow. Yellow sink set into a counter of hand-painted Mexican tile, yellow bathtub, even a yellow toilet. I balance on the yellow toilet seat now, staring into the yellow tub, where every morning my mother soaks for an hour or more, tendrils of smoke from her cigarette rising languidly into my father's towel hanging directly above. My father does not see why my mother needs to put her ashtray under *his* towel, but there is no alternative.

Outside the bathroom window I can hear birds chirping, and scratching through leaves for worms. Then the sound of the Singer starting up, the needle clicketing up and down, slow at first, then faster and faster, coming and going through my mother's growing dress.

Balanced over water, I flush. Wash my hands with the yellow soap shaped like a rosebud, dry on my mother's fresh-smelling towel.

I jump back into my nest of comfort and books by the window. My mother is whistling now, the deep full whistle of the women in her family, while yards of cloth run through her hands.

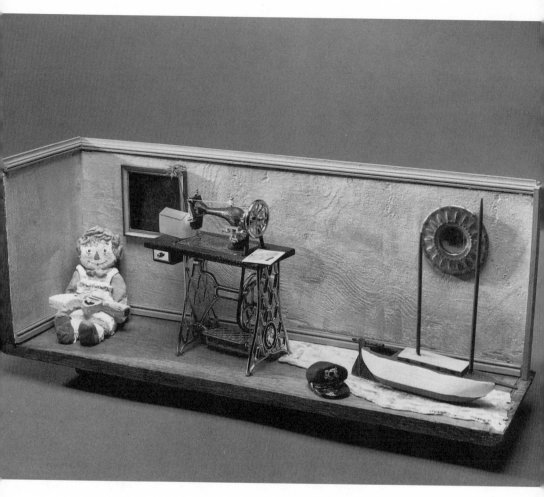

Family Room

Becky is eyeing her hamburger suspiciously. She can tell, without looking, that a fine layer of minced onions mixed with something red coats the inside of her bun. Whenever we all go to Donalee's for dinner Becky says she wants a hamburger "plain." My sister always tries to tell her the best kind of hamburger to order: mustard, mayonnaise, lettuce, tomato, pickle, cheese, sliced onions. But, no, Becky wants plain.

D I N N E R   1 9 4 4

Plain means two buns with a patty. Looking inside Becky's hamburger is like looking under a band-aid. She lifts the lid now. This time sure enough: onions, pickles, and probably catsup. She operates with her knife. Scrape, scrape, scrape across the wound. But it is clear this hamburger can never be restored.

Her brother Little Billy is eating french fries with his fingers. He likes the tiny, curled-up fries that are dark and brittle. He runs them through the pool of catsup on his plate, pretending they are cars in a flash flood.

Catherine leans back in the comfort of the big booth at Donalee's Fine Food and Drive-In, absorbed in conversation with my mother. We come here whenever both fathers, Becky's and mine, are working late and it would be silly to cook a whole dinner for just us.

It is late afternoon, and Bernice, our waitress, pulls down the filmy green shades to keep the sun out of our eyes. Hands and arms turn green. We make them move in strange ways and touch each other like blind fish. Bernice brings us milk shakes and malteds, handing us each a paper-wrapped straw and lifting her eyebrows because she knows what happens next: a blizzard of straw wrappers flying in the air.

Catherine rouses herself momentarily, snatches the straw out of Little Billy's mouth and tells him to eat his hamburger. He is still wearing the aviator helmet that keeps him from getting earaches. His skin is pale with the decision not to cry.

Little Billy never eats his hamburgers. Only a few french fries, soggy with catsup. Catherine closes her eyes now while she bites into her double decker with everything. While her eyes are squinted shut, my sister picks up Little Billy's hamburger and takes a big bite out of it for him and drops it back in his plate. Little Billy grins. Becky shoots him in the head with a straw.

We all treat Little Billy with a certain tenderness, as if we already know that when he turns eighteen, driving home alone from basic training late one night, he will plough his car into a telephone pole along some lonely stretch of Highway 1, that always emanating from him—even now—is the low irregular hum of a right front wheel spinning without purpose, suspended in moonlight.

I look up through the green film shades. Outside, the neon sign by the road has come on. Little electric arrows flicker around, directing everybody to Donalee's Fine Food.

Becky begs her mother for a nickel. She never just asks because that way Catherine can't hear. "Oh-pleaze-zo-pleaze-zo," she croons at her mother. My mother—never one to negotiate—takes out a cigarette, taps it on the Pall Mall pack, waits. Catherine hands over a nickel and finishes her sentence. My mother laughs low, coaxes ashes from the glowing tip into the green glass ash tray.

We race off to the juke box. Becky drops in the nickel and pushes G-13. The front of the machine floods with colored lights, all moving and blending and changing. We lean in close to watch the machine pick up its own tiny record. Until the sound comes out, we don't breathe. Bernice pauses, a dish towel in her hand. In the second before the record drops she sees her soldier boy standing under a Dutch windmill, sees him colored and stroked by liquid neon. Then it drops and we are all singing together the eloquent, incomprehensible words: Oh mairzy doats and dozie doats and little lambsy divey, a tiddle di didy do, wouldn't you?

Soon we will be mashed into the back seat of Catherine's ancient Ford with the tiny windows up high in the back, following our headlights up the dark hill to our houses on the horseshoe, overlooking Donalee's Fine Food. But for now Becky and my sister and I jiggle and dance and sing Oh mairzy doats and dozie doats while Little Billy—his aviator helmet askew—flutters, coughs, and purrs into action, arms outstretched like the first airplane.

TIN MAN

My mother is bending over the floor register, arranging a square of flannel so it will warm. The cloth puffs out in the stream of air. My mother sits on the side of my bed and I smell Christmas Night coming from her pressure points. When my father gets home they will go out. Probably they will dance and eat lobster.

The jar of Vicks Vaporub is the same deep blue as her bottle of Christmas Night. Slowly she unscrews the lid and dips her finger-tips into the thick pulp of eucalyptus. Then she circles my chest with her fingers, rubbing slowly, as if she has all the time in the world. I almost fall asleep. Quietly she takes the flannel from the heater and places it on my chest, tucking it in all around. My chest glows. I smell like trees.

I hear her open the closet door, turn my head to see her lift down the metal vaporizer that I hate with a passion. "You need this," she says. I close my eyes, listen to her in the kitchen running water into the hated thing. She sets it on a chair next to my bed and plugs it in. A red light like a flaming eye comes on. She waits until steam comes up and the noise begins, like restless breathing. She kisses my cheek. "Okay?" she asks. But doesn't wait. Crosses to the door and turns off the overhead light. My sister will sleep in the maid's room with Granny so my coughing won't keep her awake. I am alone with the fierce breathing and the sliver of light from the hall.

This sliver cuts across the room and paints the creature's nose and cheek in angry light. He looks now like the Tin Man might when nobody was around to see how he really was. The beam outlines the edge of the closet door and I see that it hangs open.

Open. She has forgotten, and when she has forgotten things can come out. Things.

It seems like my mother would remember something like that, as dangerous as a closet door. A mother would. And I lie in bed trying to remember the feel of her hand from before, slowly circling my chest with the Vicks, but my heart is racing and shuddering. It seems this terrible Tin Man has somehow taken away my real mother, leaving me with beautiful strangers who can dance and eat lobsters while orphans or the rightful children of royalty are devoured in the dark.

El Músico y la Dama. Exterior.

A study in light and dark, this snapshot. In the foreground a luminous birthday cake seems at first to float. Gradually the fingers of Catherine emerge from the background, gripping the giant platter. The candles have just been lit. The flames photograph dark, rather than light. Down either side of the long table, beneath a web of crepe paper streamers, child faces flicker. My sister's bandages gleam against her dark face. She is

PHOTOGRAPH 3

swathed like a mummy. A straw protrudes from a hole in the bandages, through which she drinks Hawaiian punch. She cannot open her mouth because of the bandages. Because her mouth is stitched shut. Everybody in the picture seems to be leaning forward.

Celebration does not seem to be the only motif. Perhaps Catherine leans forward to explain. Perhaps my sister leans forward to hear the explanation.

Was it Catherine who said the German shepherd next door would not bite?

Everybody agreed the chow on Indio Avenue was another story. The chow would come rattling down the length of his chain to leap out at you as you passed along the sidewalk. He seemed to shoot past himself, even: rising at the last minute like an airplane off the runway, but always always just short of you, his black tongue lolling out in disappointment.

But this dog next door to Catherine. No, this dog was not dangerous. This dog who looked like the ones you saw in newsreels trotting alongside goose-stepping soldiers. This dog was a pet, had no politics to speak of, had not and never would hurt anybody.

Who made no sudden moves. It was only necessary to move slowly and not to tease unnecessarily or by accident and not to emit any faint odor of any faint fear. Or otherwise you might fly back under the blow out of nowhere, front paws on your chest knocking you down and the teeth tearing your lips, ripping your face. But not this dog. The one not dangerous.

POCADILLAS

It is Easter morning and I wake up in my Aunt Thelma's bed. The yellow bead board ceiling is awash with light. I have slept profoundly, through the cry of the rooster and the clucking of his consorts. I am safe in my grandmother's house. The house of my mother's mother: Mymama. Della Caroline Ortiz y Cabares Shrode. Mymama.

Aunt Thelma is not in the bed. I follow the smell of coffee into my grandmother's kitchen. Mymama stands at the counter patting out giant flour tortillas. Aunt Thelma is on her third cigarette and her fourth cup of coffee. "Ia, Ia, Ia!" she exclaims, draws me toward her fragrant pajamas and pats my bottom. She and my uncle Earl have no children, live with Mymama and Mypapa, helping with the yard and the chickens, and the housekeeping in this tiny frame house near the Los Angeles River.

"You're blowing smoke in that child's face," says Mymama, flipping a tortilla over on the grill with her fingers.

"Ia, Ia, Ia," says my Aunt Thelma again, inhaling the tobacco thoughtfully, preparing to tell me again the story of my naming. "When you were a little girl and I would say to you, 'What is your name?' you'd say 'Ia, Ia, Ia.'"

"Sheila was too hard," I say.

Mymama nods, hands me a warm tortilla. "This child needs some breakfast."

"Just tortillas," I say, sitting at the long white table on the bench next to my aunt, the table Mypapa built so his thirteen children could all eat at once.

Mymama sets a thick plate before me, with tortillas rolled inside a cloth napkin. Then she takes the butter out of the ice box and puts it before me, hands me a table knife with a red handle. "For you," she says. "I always make these flour tortillas especially for you." I reach up, hugging my way into her warmth and plumpness. My cheek crushes against her cool broach, the one with the dark purple palm tree on the island, an enclosed but exotic world where I live briefly in the moments when she holds me.

There is a scraping sound from the back porch, then the slam of the screen door.

"Ovaldo," says Mymama, releasing me and wiping her hands on a dishtowel.

He appears in the doorway, her brother, her male double. Both short, brown, low centers of gravity, curly and rebellious gray hair, a certain seriousness, a certain weight, a certain amused light now and then escaping from dark eyes, the eyes of their mother, Teresa Cabares, whose people came from Morelia, the city of beautiful women.

"*Traigo el maíz,*" he says. Under his left arm he carries a rough bundle of corn wrapped in funny papers and in his right hand he carries a bouquet of irises wrapped in waxed paper and secured at the stems with a red rubber band.

"Well how are you, Uncle O.V.?" says my Aunt Thelma, without the slightest expectation of a reply. My mother says he is deaf as a door post. My father says he doesn't speak English. Mymama has told me he lives in his own world.

His own world is two streets over. He lives there with his

daughter Sonna and her husband, two boys and fifteen cats. In the front yard are decaying cars—doors fallen off, windows out, rumble seats swollen and split—which Sonna has planted with geraniums that cascade out windows and doors and into the yard. Flowers everywhere.

My uncle nods at Thelma as she takes the twin bouquets from his arms, then turns to go. Mymama follows him out, murmuring in Spanish.

At the sink my aunt rips off the corn husks, rinses corn and husks under the tap. Later my mother will come, and Aunt Maggie and Aunt Frances and Aunt Julia, and they will stand in a line making Easter tamales and laughing and telling stories. My Aunt Thelma whistles as she works, deep and loud like my mother. She is in her own world. I move off to the living room to study Mymama's *pocadillas*.

Mymama's *pocadillas* are arranged along three long glass shelves. They are tiny and require frequent dusting. Mostly they are things people have brought her: pin cushions and tiny tea pots that are really salt and pepper shakers. A ceramic seal balancing a ball on his nose. My mother says they all have a story. I touch the glass dog, the one my Uncle David gave her when he was seven years old and had not yet blown off the two fingers on his left hand with a dynamite cap. I touch the glass dog and hear the marimba band that was playing on Olvera Street when the old glassblower put his lips to the pipe.

Next to this is a chartreuse ceramic ashtray my sister made in first grade by tracing around an ivy leaf and pressing its intricate veins into wet clay. I turn it over to see her initials: ST. An elephant tusk comes next. It is carved in the shape of a snake and has

Pocadillas

secret drawers lined in green felt that we are not supposed to open. I ease one out to see the tiny game pieces and hear the Chinese music, then slide it closed. A German medal lies next to the tusk. Uncle Arthur captured it and sent it home with a silk pillow that says Guam. I trace the map, hear rifle fire.

Next come three tiny bottles of perfume from Mexico. My great grandfather Miguel brought these to my great grandmother Teresa when he took his first business trip to Mexico City after their marriage. It is said my great grandmother was still a child, and that when he asked her what she would like him to bring her she asked for a doll. I hold the golden bottle up close to my eye; it is half full but still sealed tight.

I stop, the bottle warm in my hand. I hear voices. Beyond the front porch I see Mymama and her brother talking together, their heads close. Between them and me, hanging in the front window, are a blue cloth panel embroidered with seven gold service stars—one for each uncle—and a blue cardboard sign asking for ten pounds of ice.

CONVOY

My mother is sitting on the couch examining a dust mop. Across from her sits the Fuller Brush Man. I sit on the corn goddess rug between them, playing with a vegetable brush. The Fuller Brush Man's black case is open on the floor. He holds glossy books on his knees. My mother keeps adjusting the neck of her house dress, which inclines to fall open just below the lace of her slip. The Fuller Brush Man, with his twice a year visits, always surprises her. She is often not quite dressed. She must throw a house dress on, appear, as she puts it, "without her face."

But this purchasing of brushes is serious. It requires black cases, shiny books, forms that must be checked off, signed, torn along perforations. These are supplies that must be had. Like the sailors in newsreels, we need things that must be brought to us, against great odds. Like them, we are at sea.

My mother does not drive. My father says it is not necessary. Twice a week my mother pulls me in the Radio Flyer down Indio Avenue to the Mixville Market. Otherwise supplies are brought in. On Mondays and Wednesdays the Helms Bakery Man comes in his yellow and blue truck. We climb inside while he slides out large, fragrant wooden drawers of backed goods. He lifts cookies, coffee cakes, cupcakes, brownies in squares of waxed paper, places everything carefully in white bags. He keeps his change in a machine on his belt. He flips the lever with his thumb and dimes flicker into his palm. We run into the house with our white parcels, laughing, smelling of bread.

Every other Thursday the Date Man comes. He rocks along the dirt road in his Model A truck, dust clouds streaming behind, scale clanking, isinglass windows winking in the California sunshine. We crowd around, fingering plums, dates, grapes. His scale is a miracle of tin, chain, arrow and dial. My mother lifts a cluster of dates, slides them into the brown bag he holds. His dry, tortoise neck rises out of a high collar. He must be a hundred years old. Old as raisins.

The Fuller Brush Man is younger. His hair is thick and blond. A flaxen moustache covers his lip. From living in the presence of brushes he has begun to sprout them. He tells jokes, asks my mother if he can take off his coat. It's that warm.

She opens the french doors. I think of the joke my father tells, the one I don't understand, where he lifts me up in his arms, strokes my blond hair, says to my mother, "Must have been the Fuller Brush Man."

AND THE SKIES ARE NOT

I am standing before an easel wearing one of my father's soft and sweet-smelling dress shirts backwards. I dip my fat brush into a can of blue calcimine paint and streak it across the top of my rippling paper.

At last I am in school, Allesandro Street School, the only school in the city named for an Indian. I have waited five years for this day, the day when I would walk to school with my sister along the winding streets, down the steep concrete steps, across the Red Car tracks, across this territory that the Mexican government granted my great grandfather Miguel Ortiz for an obscure favor performed long ago, land subsequently lost to the family out of a certain characteristic vagueness about property and ownership.

I breathe in the warm chaos of Mrs. Gordon's kindergarten class. Behind me children build rooms out of giant wood blocks, others sing, others recite their alphabet. I paint, streaking my sky, this picture shaping itself from top to bottom.

"What are you doing?" asks the girl next to me in a tone I have never heard before but will in time become familiar with. "Skies aren't stuck up at the top. They come all the way down to here." She bends over, indicating to me the tops of her ruffled socks.

I stop my work, looking from the girl's socks to the top of my picture.

"Does not," says the girl on my other side. I look over gratefully. She has deep dark eyes, straight black hair. Her eyes say it has cost her something to contradict this girl who knows everything. Her name is Hazel Medina. I fall in love with her, then and there. Hazel Medina.

"And skin color," says the first girl, "this is skin color for when you make people." She moves a can of calcimine from her easel to mine. I look into the can. The paint is the color of pale seafood sauce. I decide never to paint people. Oceans, maybe. Or deserts.

"Time for music," calls Mrs. Gordon. "Bring your chairs into a circle, here, around the piano."

I stand with my brush poised. Hazel Medina shows me how to set the brushes into jars of water. We take off our father's shirts and pull chairs up near the piano. Then the first girl pulls her chair up on my other side. She is wearing a new plaid school dress that has a little white apron attached. She smoothes it carefully. A large white bow holds her hair in place. The teacher keeps calling her Eleanor dear.

We are halfway through "Little Wind Blow on the Hilltop" when my vaccination starts itching. I look up high on my left arm where a scab has formed. Now that I have looked at it, thinking of anything else becomes impossible.

It looks like a dormant volcano; black, ashen, and very, very dangerous. Eleanor dear looks also. She gives a little shudder of disgust, turns back, straightens the starched white apron part of her dress. Red Buster Brown sandals form a grid over her ruffled socks. I examine these socks once more to see if blue sky comes all the way down. Then I check Eleanor dear's arm for a vaccination. Nothing. Then I look out the window.

When we finish "Little Wind Blow on the Hilltop," Mrs. Gordon tells us we have a treat because Eleanor Manning plays the violin. She gestures with her hand and says "Eleanor dear," as if it is an invitation.

Eleanor Manning gets up, smoothes her white apron, and accepts an enormous violin case from Mrs. Gordon. This violin case looks like my Uncle Jake's coffin, even to the pale blue velvet inside. I see my Aunt Thelma reaching inside to pick up Uncle Jake's pale, slender hand to pat it in consolation. Eleanor Manning reaches inside and extracts a gleaming violin and a tiny velvet pillow. She puts the tiny pillow under her chin and nestles the violin on top of it. Eleanor Manning draws her bow across the violin and adjusts the tuning. I feel a ragged pain in a back tooth each time Eleanor Manning moves the bow.

The itching in my vaccination becomes more intense. I look over at Hazel Medina, who is staring out the window thinking of home. I glance around the room for evidence this violin playing has set off an itching in everybody's vaccinations. Nobody could come to school without these vaccinations, my mother has said, and yet no one else seems to be driven half crazy like me.

Eleanor Manning plays "Twinkle, Twinkle Little Star" through twice, then puts away her violin and then the tiny pillow, snaps the case shut and hands it back to Mrs. Gordon. She returns to the chair next to mine, arranges her white apron.

Mrs. Gordon says, "Thank you Eleanor. Wasn't that just wonderful, people?"

At last I scratch this left arm of mine, defying my father's express command: I might scar myself for life if I scratch. Nevertheless, I scratch. Relief and well-being suffuse me. When Mrs. Gordon passes around the triangles, sandpaper blocks, maracas, and tambourines I reach happily for a beautiful polished block with a padded drum stick. I touch the block softly with the stick in my right hand and send out into the air a melodious tree sound; this is the meaning of the word *forest*. I glance sideways at Eleanor Manning, violinist. Then I see it: in the exact middle of Eleanor Manning's white apron rests the black scab of my vaccination. I stop breathing.

The others are all singing "Home, Home on the Range" and hitting wood blocks and triangles. Eleanor Manning sings, her head lightly tilted back, her eyes half closed. I close my own, and join my voice with hers and with Hazel Medina's. We sing through to the end, joy and confusion bubbling inside me, until Mrs. Gordon collects the rhythm instruments and tells us the first day of school is over.

We jump up, run outside. My mother stands in the schoolyard waiting under a eucalyptus tree, the bright California sky floating over her head like a blue banner.

LATTICEWORK

It is Saturday morning. My mother is paring apples over the kitchen sink. An empty pie crust waits. The oven ticks with preheating. My sister stands on a chair rolling out dough to make pie crust people. Dreamily, standing on a stool next to my mother, I turn the green, wooden handle on the sifter. I make a shush, shush sound—like when my father does soft shoe on the wooden floor of the hall.

My mother arranges the sliced apples into the pie shell. "Oops," she says, handing me a pale plastic square of uncolored Nucoa. "Almost forgot this."

I begin squeezing the bag of wartime margarine, blending and squishing the orange pellet of color through the white lard. At first it streaks like a sunset, then under the warmth of my hand re-laxes into a uniform lemon yellow. My sister is practicing her art, cutting people out of dough, bronzing them with cinnamon and sugar. She works with concentration. My mother sugars the ap-ples, reaches for the bag of Nucoa, pauses.

Through the kitchen window we see my father approach the olive tree. He has a step ladder in the crook of his arm, a saw in his hand. He positions the ladder, tests it. Leaves. Returns with a small can of paint, which he places at the base of the tree.

My mother holds the bag of Nucoa suspended. My father mounts the ladder and begins sawing with even strokes. Letting the blade do the work. There is no need to apply pressure when cutting correctly. The teeth track and retrack, slipping into a groove of their own making.

A blue jay dive bombs his head. He throws up an arm. Protects the tender part of his head where nothing will grow.

My mother cuts open the bag of Nucoa with her kitchen scis-sors and begins dotting the slices of apple.

The limb falls. My father backs down the ladder, disappears.

My mother sprinkles cinnamon over the apples. Steps back.

My father is crouched under the olive tree, prying at the small
can of paint with a screw driver.

My mother takes the remaining pie dough from my sister and rolls it vigorously, evenly, into a perfect circle.

My father dips his brush into the paint can, mounts the ladder, protecting his head from the jay.

From the circle of dough my mother cuts long strips, lays them across the pie, building lattice.

Where the limb had been, my father applies white paint, thoughtfully, in a circle.

In a pie tin, my mother lays out my sister's dough art. She listens to the temperature of the oven, holding her head momentarily tilted like a listening bird. Hearing a perfect 350, she slides in the two pie tins.

My father descends the ladder.

My father is reading the morning paper aloud to my mother, using the tone of voice that means if anybody ever bothered to listen to him we all could save ourselves a world of trouble.

"No," says my mother, blotting her red mouth on the cloth napkin, "it was not horse meat."

I crane my head over my father's bent arm to see what he sees. It's a picture of Mr. Kasirian, the nice butcher who never asks my mother for her meat rationing coupons when we buy our steaks from him. He is smiling, holding out pristine white packages of meat, taped nicely with the butcher's tape he sometimes lets me reel off the dispenser while he talks to my mother.

DINNER 1945

My father gives her the look that means she would not know horse meat if it whinnied at her, but he forbears.

"Mr. Kasirian was a very nice man," says my mother, as if he were dead. My mother has the democratic belief that most shopkeepers are basically honest and the elitist belief that they prefer her to all their other customers. "Mr. Kasirian would never have sold me horse meat."

"Well, personally, I liked it," says my father, taking a sudden mental detour, and shaking the *Times* open to the next page. He is five years from his first heart attack and has a sanguine attitude toward the consumption of flesh. "I don't know what we'll do now."

"I'll go to Mixville," says my mother.

The Mixville Market is down the hill from us. My mother has a friendly feeling for Mixville because it is named for Tom Mix, the famous western movie actor. My mother and all her brothers and sisters acted in these movies, playing children in crowd scenes. They all remember fondly the huge, hot meals served out of the back of a chuck wagon. My mother could have had a wonderful career in the movies. So she likes to shop at Mixville Market even though she has to walk there, pulling my sister and me behind her in the Radio Flyer.

My father, however, has certain apprehensive feelings toward the butcher at the Mixville Market. Until five minutes ago he had those same apprehensions about Mr. Kasirian, for whose horse meat steaks he is beginning to feel a faint sense of nostalgia. He will never find steaks as good as those horse meat ones, he's convinced. "I don't know what we'll do now," he says again, and heaves a sigh. My father's moon is in Cancer and he tends toward melancholia at times.

My mother gives him a look of total incomprehension and grinds her cigarette into the yolk of her cold egg, a gesture that almost always provokes in my father a barely suppressed shudder.

"I'll just go to Mixville," she repeats.

"Kasirian's the only man who knew meat," pronounces my father gloomily, averting his gaze from the egg.

"We could have chicken," reminds my mother. "If I could drive." Silence falls. My father has gone to considerable trouble and expense to buy these five lots on the top of this hill almost overlooking beautiful Silver Lake. He has built this fine house and now his wife is always laying plans to leave it. He takes a cigarette. He only has five more years before the doctors forbid him to smoke, but he does not know this.

"The chickens at Mixville are not fit to eat," says my mother.

"I know that," he says.

The grownups have reached an impasse. Finally I say, "We could go with Catherine." They look up.

Personally I hate chicken. I tend to associate chickens with death. My Aunt Thelma raises chickens, and though she loves them and calls them "the girls" Monday through Saturday, on

Sundays she wrings their necks with all the good will in the world, two at a time, swinging their bodies in opposite directions.

It is my father's theory that they feel nothing.

My mother, who probably has wrung the necks of a few chickens in her time, prefers to buy her chickens from the poultry store off Atwater, where assassination is a service included in the price of the chicken.

Over the telephone, later in the morning, my mother puts it to Catherine: "Let's buy a nice chicken." She always refers to living creatures intended for our dinner as "nice," as if in apology for their sacrifice. An hour later we are standing in the poultry store, Mother, Catherine, Becky, and I. Cages are stacked to the ceiling. Heads of every description—brown, black, white, black and white —thrust through the wire and cocks' combs shake inquisitively, furiously, asking questions in a clucking tongue. There is beneath the counting sound, an undertone of whuffling feathers and an aroma of grain and blood.

Our mothers run practiced eyes over the gallery of hens while Becky and I step outside to see the baby ducks in a pen on the sidewalk. Six or seven are searching through ripped up newspaper as if they believe bugs will emerge on the streets of Los Angeles. The morose-looking duck standing in the pie tin of murky water catches my eye. He seems to be looking at me. With a little wire and a cardboard box I could make him comfortable. Build him a little pond, maybe. Teach him to come when I called.

My mother appears in the doorway of the shop holding a white, oblong parcel. From one end of the wrapping a grizzled foot protrudes. My mother looks from me to the foot and from the foot to me. In the silence we listen to the blank sound of passing cars. When I ask her for the duck, she nods. Catherine's mouth falls open against her white chins. She and my mother have a pact against pets. For years they have said no dogs, cats outside, maybe. Now the poultry man picks up the duck from the dish of water, absently wipes one hand against his red apron, smiles. He is staring at Catherine. Becky is looking up at her in that pleading way I know for a fact she practices in the mirror. Finally Catherine nods, and the man picks up a second duckling. On the way home Becky and I, breathless, take turns holding the brown bag with the two breathing ducks. In the front seat the mothers say nothing.

Training the duck is not easy. In war newsreels I have seen countless pigeons trained to fly hundreds of miles, through storms and enemy gunfire, carrying tiny messages in capsules strapped to their legs. But whenever I lift my duck over the wire enclosure and set him down, he swivels his head in all directions and sets out for Mixville. I chase behind him, calling, carry him home. As he grows taller he becomes more self-assured. One day he bites my hands. I drop him. We stand there looking at each other in the field of winter weeds. He turns toward Mixville. I can't leave him. There are cats, owls, dogs. It's not safe. He stretches his neck in his stubborn innocence. I pick him up and run again toward home until the biting hurts too much, drop him again, run again until the biting begins.

The next day he is gone, escaped from his pen. I find him a block from Mixville, hurrying as if late for an appointment. He is furious with me, bites my hands, wrists, forearms. I drop him hard this time. Slowly we make our way home in a strange and halting dance.

This time my mother has been watching from the window, makes up her mind. The duck will go live with Aunt Thelma's chickens.

On the first visit, my duck runs over to the wire almost as if he recognizes me. The second visit, he is lost in a sea of hens, a tall white sculpted face, waiting.

Easter comes. My uncles line up at the kitchen sink and toss back shots of tequila. Crocks of chicken enchiladas dot the table, baskets of fragrant tortillas folded into cloth napkins, steaming tamales with sweet, hot raisins concealed inside. We sit at the long table, children first, adults later because we are so many. Across from us sits Aunt Ella, who always eats through both sittings. She is big as a monument, eats slow and steady. My older cousins giggle when she reaches her ponderous arm forth to scoop more enchiladas. We laugh too and squirm, watch butter melt on the fresh tortillas Mymama has made.

Finally we stand to change places, grownups settling down on the benches, children released into spring air. My sister and I bang out the screen door into the back yard, free and running toward the coop, raising dust like wild mustangs, and with the striking of each heel in the soft dirt understanding a little better; and better still; and better still—so that by the time we hit the fence we already know.

ELECTRICITY TREE

It's Saturday morning and my sister is drizzling pancake batter onto the griddle in the shape of an S for Sandra. I am buttering a leaning stack of silver dollar pancakes. There must be twenty of them. My mother is heating Log Cabin syrup that actually comes in a log cabin. My father walks through the kitchen saying good morning to nobody. My mother wants to look up but does not. We call this The Silent Treatment. This is what they do instead of yell.

My sister and I are not supposed to fight either. Be nice, she says, you're all you have. Like we are orphans. Whenever she leaves the house, walks down the horseshoe to see Catherine, we jump out at each other and hit fast and hard in the arm, getting in every lick stacked up inside us like dollar pancakes, and we do this until she comes back or my nose bleeds.

My sister flips her pancake over and now it is a backward S. My mother pours the syrup into a little pitcher because no containers must be on the table, even if they look like log cabins. Of course, she never eats breakfast. When we sit down with our pancakes and milk, she sits down too, pulling the ashtray in front of her like it is a plate of bacon. She sips coffee, smokes. Then she says it, "I want you girls to go to Mixville for me."

Simple enough on the surface, but we have never gone to Mixville Market alone before. My sister looks up with a white moustache, her brows darkening like the winter sky.

"Your father wants a *Reader's Digest* and you can bring me a magazine too. Pick one out for me." She breathes in hard on her Pall Mall. My father walks through the dining room but does not speak.

She does not say the real thing until she is zipping up my jacket, kneeling, as she does to be close. "We might go live with My-mama for a while, just us, not Daddy." She gives us a dollar apiece, four quarters tied up safe in hankies and pinned to our jackets. Then we are out the door.

Somehow I have forgotten to strap on my guns but I don't really want to go back in for them. My sister has her Dick Tracy handcuffs, but otherwise we are unarmed. I start to cut across the field, but my sister stops me. She heads for the garage, and at first I don't know what she's looking for. Then I see it, my father's For Sale By Owner sign, still leaning just inside the door, my grandmother's old Victrola almost covering it. When the sign goes up in front of the house that means we are about to move to Mexico or even sail around the world and so should not get too involved, like when my sister wanted to join Girl Scouts.

Relieved, we head for the short cut, jumping off the retaining wall, into tall winter rye. We walk single file past the baseball diamond, and cut through the policeman's back yard, coming out onto Indio Avenue and the Star House Movers.

My father hates it that Star House Movers is in this residential neighborhood, but I like it. Sometimes they keep houses here that are sawed in half and up on giant blocks. You can see inside like you're at a play. Then the men put them on their big trucks and take them off in pieces. My father thinks all this is unsightly and noisy but it certainly is interesting. Like today there is the back half of a yellow house and you can see into the kitchen and two bedrooms. The bathroom is split right along the bath tub. A man in a ball cap is leaning under the hood of one of the trucks and keeps making the engine roar from outside, where he is standing. We watch for awhile, then head down Indio Avenue toward Mixville.

Oh, we know the way all right. Mother has pulled us on the Radio Flyer since I was born. You might say I know every crack on the sidewalk. But even though the way is shorter, she never cuts through the Silver Lake Auto Court, maybe because of my father's war with them.

They make more noise than the Star House Movers. It's because of the telephone. There must be at least a hundred people living in there and they don't have phones, so every time it rings in the office a man or a woman says over the microphone, "Mrs. Amwell in Trailer Number 44, please come to the telephone." I hardly notice it at all but my father does. It makes him watchful and at night he hardly can sleep at all. Sometimes he calls them on the phone, my mother says. Sometimes he calls the police.

We stand outside the fence of the Silver Lake Auto Court. There are lots of thick plants, so it's hard to see inside. We think about going in, cutting through. Just inside the entrance is a silvery trailer with a canvas awning and green metal chairs. A woman thick as Aunt Ella is bent over a washtub with her back to us. I feel like I want to sit in one of the green chairs, to see inside the trailer. My sister is sniffing the air. She has the Ortiz nose. I don't have it yet.

"Gasoline," she says. I know about gasoline from the books my sister reads me about the people who live on a farm with collies. Somebody is always trying to burn down their farm with gasoline because they are jealous of the dogs and the quiet life. Dogs bark just in time, warning the people. My sister lifts her nose like a collie about to bark. "She's washing clothes in gasoline," she says in a way the woman can't hear. She says this like the woman is breaking a law.

"Why?" I ask.

"Instead of dry cleaning," she explains, but I don't really understand.

From her back pocket she takes a booklet. I see that under her unzipped jacket she is wearing her Jr. Fire Department badge. She earned this special chief's badge by writing out citations for Catherine, whose house had more fire hazards than anybody else on the horseshoe. Without Catherine my sister could not have earned this gold badge.

She is reading from the Jr. Fire Department official booklet. "Yes," she confirms, "it's a six-point fire hazard. That woman could explode any minute."

"What should we do?" I say.

"We could explode too," my sister says with satisfaction. Then she writes a citation out of the coupons at the back and sets it carefully on the green chair. When we leave the woman is still washing the clothes.

A little path winds through the rest of the trailer park. The trailers are up close to each other. I can hear sounds of silverware and sometimes a radio playing music. In a window a gray cat is curled, its eyes opening and closing softly. An old lady in red shoes and a shawl sits outside with a Chihuahua in her lap. She feeds the little dog chocolates from a white box, a piece at a time. There is a green luxury here. I might want to live in a silver trailer one day with my sister and let them call me to the phone. I almost don't want to leave, but we are through the other side.

The Mixville Market smells like ripe cantaloupe, bananas on the brink. Ralph, the produce man, waves at us. We don't go in.

On the other side of the market is the drug store. I always get this funny feeling right outside the drug store because I used to dream I flew here and that everybody came outside to see the flying girl and talked and laughed and pointed. I used to believe one day I would fly and that I'd go straight to the Mixville Drug Store and everybody would come out and I'd be floating around like a balloon just smiling and pretending this was an everyday thing, a girl flying.

Inside, we go straight to the magazine rack. There's a new *Little Lulu* and a *Captain Marvel*. My sister likes *Classic Comics* but they are too hard to read. She chooses one called *Great Expectations* and also a *Superman,* just to be on the safe side. I get the *Little Lulu* and a *Reader's Digest* for my father, because I like to read them when he's finished. One day I will send *Reader's Digest* a joke and make fifty dollars. We get Mother a *Vogue,* for the fashion, and hand over the money from our hankies to the cash register lady, who knows us and probably thinks Mother is next door at the market. There is enough left over for a Nehi for me and a Mars Bar for my sister.

The bag is heavy. We start back, the usual way, down the sidewalk. For a while we pretend we are horses and then we slow down, thinking about going to live with Mymama. The sky is clouding over again. If it rains we decide we'll run to the Electricity Tree and stay inside until they call us, or maybe forever.

We really could live there. I don't see why not. It's this burnt-out tree, struck by lightning. We actually saw it on fire. There were fire trucks and everybody on the horseshoe came out and stood in the sprinkling rain telling about how they were the first to see it but it was really Little Billy, who ran home screaming to Catherine, "Mama, Mama, the moke is getting toser and toser."

Now we have it all fixed up as our tree house and Green Lantern Club. Inside we have real light switches screwed into the tree walls, and electrical plugs, and bright colored wires strung around —all things the workmen left when the Bancarrols added a garage. Nothing they wanted anymore. Outside we wrapped tar paper around and around the tree and then nailed on a roll of chicken wire to hold it. When we go inside we always check to make sure nothing has been touched. Once boys broke in and stole our comic books, two perfectly good flares we had found beside the Red Car tracks, and the green lantern we were going to use for night meetings someday when we got some matches.

But today everything is just the way we left it. My sister sets down the sack from the drug store, pulls the tar paper door closed, and we sit down cross-legged on a nest of comic books.

Because this great burnt-out tree is eucalyptus everything smells like charcoal and Vicks Vaporub when your mother rubs it on your chest. I open my Nehi with the opener hanging from a nail over my head and my sister peels the wrapper from her Mars Bar. After awhile she gets thirsty and I get hungry, so we swap off, not saying much, just listening to raindrops tapping the tar paper roof, lightly, like the sound of my grandmother's short brown fingers on the table top whenever my mother lights a cigarette. It would be okay to go there, we decide, to live for awhile.

Then my sister picks up the book she is reading to me, *Running Away with Nebby*. It's about this horse who gets old and so the grown-ups decide to take him to the glue factory, which means to kill him, so the kids run away with old Nebby and of course have adventures, like we did this very day with the Star House Movers and Silver Lake Auto Court and going to Mixville alone. I lean back against the tree trunk, listening to my sister's voice and to the drumming of the rain on our roof.

FRONT AND CENTER

Becky's father is leaning over my bike bolting a tiny red trailer to the back. Thinning red hair floats over his forehead like a halo as he tightens with his wrench. "There," he says, stepping back to admire.

Becky's father is a carpenter and keeps building on rooms to the house. When he is not doing that, or away working somewhere, then he is making these trailers for the backs of kids' bikes. Becky and I are going to pull our trailers through the neighborhood and then eventually everybody will want to buy one and Becky and her family will get rich. Big Bill says that's what America is all about.

Becky pulls alongside my rig, her trailer filled with dolls, a bag of dog biscuits, and her painted turtle. "Thanks Bill," I say, dropping my jacket into my new trailer and climbing onto my bike.

"Just a minute, young lady," says Catherine, peering around the side of the garage at Becky. "You're not going anywhere until you clean your room." Catherine must still be mad about the chocolates. Her Mrs. See's Finest Assortment. The ones she keeps up high in the hall closet. We get them down when she's gone for any length of time and lie across Becky's Old Folks at Home four-poster bed, sticking toothpicks into the bottoms of her chocolates to see if they are worth eating. We used to just hold them up to a light bulb but you can't tell as much that way. Anything with pistachio nuts, for example, is not worth the spanking that Becky will probably get if we are caught.

"I'll be right back," Becky says. "You wait." I rest on my bike. Then I ease it forward a little. The trailer follows. A miracle of invention.

Big Bill is bending over a giant work table made of sawhorses. He is carefully varnishing little slats for the sides of the trailers. Sometimes from my bed at night I look out the window and see the sparklers and blue light from his welding torch. Another table holds all the red wheels. The rubber from them smells good. Everything so clean. Clean rubber. Clean red. Red as fire engines, everywhere you look. I bend my head up, and see them. Hundreds, maybe thousands of red trailers hanging in rows from the garage ceiling. Every week, more trailers.

"I can't go," snuffles Becky, suddenly appearing.

Her father looks up in mild concern, but he'll never say anything. He turns back to his varnishing.

"I talked back," she says, then stifles a giggle.

I take the long way home so more people can see my trailer and want to buy one. Slowly I pedal along the horseshoe, keeping my eyes straight ahead, like a red bike trailer is an everyday thing for me. When I turn into the driveway my father is stacking boxes all over the garage.

"Bill make that?" he asks, stopping to mop his forehead with his hanky and slide his glasses back up on his nose.

"He's going to sell these trailers to everybody and make a lot of money," I say, climbing off my bike.

He bends close to see. "Nice workmanship," he says.

"What're you doing? What's in the boxes?" I ask.

"Well," he says, squatting down next to Big Bill's trailer, "you know how sometimes when you go into a store nobody notices you've come in and you just have to stand around waiting? I mean, it's a terrible waste of time." He seems to have gotten mad just thinking about nobody waiting on him, even though he is standing right here, in our own garage. I'm not sure what to say. He stands up eventually and goes back to stacking the boxes, as if he's alone in the garage.

"Yes," I say.

Then he stops stacking the boxes and opens one up, gestures for me to come over and look. Inside is a new black rubber door mat with a thick electrical cord and wires running to a white plastic box with musical notes embossed on it. The whole thing looks like a bomb from a Flash Gordon movie. My father beams at me.

"What's that?" I say.

"You know how when you go to a hotel and the bell captain wants a bell hop he'll call, 'Front and center'?" My father has been getting louder and by the time he gets to the words "front and center" I give a little jump of surprise. Besides, I have never been in a hotel in my life.

I nod.

"Well, that's what I'm calling it." He waits. Mrs. Bancarrol drives by with her car full of dogs in bandannas. Then it's quiet.

Finally he says, "Look," and takes the door mat out of the box and lays it out on the garage floor; also the white plastic box with the musical notes. "Every small business in this country's going to want one of these. Every big business too. Then we can retire early and move to Mexico." He plugs the cords from the mat and from the white box into an electrical outlet. "Now step on the mat," he says. "Just casually."

"What?"

"Step on it."

Electricity has always frightened me. My family has a troubled relationship with sources of energy and light.

"Go ahead," he urges, a current coming out of him and into me.

When I step on the mat, chimes sound and rebound in our garage and inside my head.

"That's it!" my father exclaims in the tone of someone who has just finished telling a long, complicated joke but it's been worth it. "That's it! Front and Center!"

By the time we stack up the last of the boxes in the garage, except for the dozen or so he puts in his car to give away to businesses as free samples, the chime from the kitchen sounds in the garage. Mother must want us to come in for dinner. We step back to look at our work. In the dim overhead light the boxes look almost exactly like a castle with high turrets. I pull my rig in tight next to the boxes, then follow my father into the house.

LIVES OF BUTTERFLIES

This is the day of the butterfly funeral. My sister is fitting up a Diamond match box, gluing on red and yellow rickrack from the bottom drawer of my mother's Singer sewing machine. Everything

is spread out over the playing surface of the Ping-Pong table. If my father comes home before she is done he will call this "scissors and paste." Inside the box is a little pink square of satin. The monarch butterfly lies on top, entirely still, one of his fine velvet wings a little ragged now. All around the table purple-blue blossoms have drifted down from the jacaranda tree and my sister moves back and forth, stepping carefully on them so they will not crush and become slippery. In her moving she looks like the St. Teresa priest on Easter Sunday, everything purple and solemn.

Just beyond the dining room window is our burial ground. Toby is there. And Duke. The baby possum that got run over by Mrs. Wood when she went crazy. And the hummingbird Duke ate when she was going to have kittens. But mostly butterflies.

We all should try to think of the lives of butterflies, my father says, who has read about them in both *Readers' Digest* and the *Encyclopedia Britannica* from the library. They have only one month to live—no more—and that is why it is very important not to collect them in jars with holes punched in the lids, even if you put grass in. Because how would you like it.

Since understanding this my sister especially has decorated these boxes in colorful ways and asked Big Bill to come up from Becky's house to dig a deep hole in the hard ground around our house. It was Big Bill who believed Becky when she said her painted turtle was not dead, just tired. He put it in the sun and drew little marks around all four feet so we would know if it was moving. It stayed there three days and then we had the funeral at our house.

Pretty soon Becky will come with a couple of Eskimo Pie sticks for the cross. I lean over my sister's shoulder to see the beautiful box. Then, in the silence of our watching we suddenly hear Daddy's car in the garage. My sister looks at me with her dark eyes. It's early, for him. We start putting things away, the scissors and paste.

But there is too much and the next thing we know he is already out of his car, standing on the top step of the patio, just looking. Looking, looking, looking. Finally he says he will get his shovel. He never does this.

Usually my sister puts on one of Daddy's ties for the funeral but decides not to risk it today. We wait. Becky arrives with the cross, snapping the red rubber band in place. Daddy comes back carrying his shovel, still wearing his brown lawyer pants and wing tip shoes. His tie is loose and hangs down his shirt front.

The four of us walk single file around to the burial ground, Becky carrying the cross but not daring to sing "Jesus Wants Me for a Sunbeam" the way she usually does. And no candles because when we buried the canary last month Becky set her bangs on fire and got a spanking. We tell my father about making the grave deep on account of what we learned when Lulubelle got dug up that one time. Since we are shy and embarrassed at having Daddy with us instead of at work where he belongs we don't talk, even though my sister has a way with words and usually makes a little speech or reads us a poem.

My father stands in the sunshine leaning on his shovel, a mild breeze lifting his handsome hair up off his bald spot for just a second. We all seem to be waiting for something to happen. Someone should say something. Something about the brief life of butterflies. But the only sound is the vague, sustained humming from the high-tension tower in the vacant lot next to us.

BOOK TWO

BLACK IRIS

My Aunt Pearl is running through the irises, naked as the morning, as if she were twenty again, running like a long-distance runner, as if she has a long way to go, as if she does not anticipate that in five minutes her neighbor to the north will catch a glimpse of her out her kitchen window, her fallen flying breasts setting the rhythm for her stride, does not anticipate the neighbor dialing the phone as she watches through the window, does not see her calling my Uncle Arthur at work to say Pearl's really gone this time, you better come home and catch her.

My Aunt Pearl is running as if her life depended on it, sprinting through this pinwheeling field of her own irises, planted with her own hands, deep velvet purple, yellow with streaks of rust, white parchment with rivers of blue; running from the house and Uncle Arthur and the three yapping Boston terriers—all of whom she loves but must run from as if her life depended; each foot hitting the earth between the rows with the same determination she brought to the task of producing the black iris, then rows of them, the black extravagant improbabilities toward which she now runs.

In this one my Uncle Jimmy Doll, wearing his navy dress uniform, is seated in the doorway of a black limousine, his head between his knees. My mother, in a hat that looks like a crow poised for flight, bends over him. Others stand aside to give him air.

This is his wedding picture.

Uncle Jimmy Doll is not marrying Rosie Capuccio. Instead he is marrying a round-faced woman who packs hamburger buns at Van de Kamps bakery, a woman known as Molly B.

P H O T O G R A P H   4

Jimmy Doll is my mother's youngest brother, the youngest of all thirteen children, so naturally when he came home from war his seven brothers wanted to tell him exactly what to do instead of going to beauty school. My mother thought he should do what he wanted, especially if what he wanted was artistic. They are both artistic and look almost exactly alike, like Spanish dancers. So instead of going to beauty school Jimmy Doll is working at Van de Kamps—where most of my family works—as a baker, which is what he was in the navy. Jimmy Doll met Molly B in hamburger buns, and according to my Aunt Thelma, Molly B tracked Jimmy Doll down like he was a deer.

This is my first wedding.

I am standing next to my father and wearing a pale yellow dotted swiss dress that scratches under the arms. We are all gathered outside St. Teresa's until my uncle gets his breath back. Mymama is dressed in black and has a veil over her face. So far the wedding feels a lot like Uncle Jake's funeral two years ago, the same combination of festivity and disaster.

Molly B, in her floating wedding dress and her hair dressed high on her head, circulates, tossing her coif back to laugh now and then. This hair is bright red, dyed by my Uncle Jimmy Doll himself, practicing his art in the only way left to him. The catsup red of her hair draws attention to the similarity between Molly B's face and the hamburger buns she packs five days a week in Van de Kamps bakery.

I look over at Jimmy Doll. My mother is rubbing his back in slow circles. He lifts his head momentarily, his face the color of dough, then lowers it. My father is discussing marriage and divorce law with my two uncles who have refused to marry their common-law wives. The one on my father's right is called Brother and has a purple face. He is six foot five. His spouse, laughing now with Molly B, is four foot eight and looks like a country western singer. My mother always refers to her as Crazy Rena, with an odd mixture of contempt and admiration in her voice. Their two sons are named Elmer David and David Elmer, after my grandfather. When Crazy Rena calls them home—Elmer David, David Elmer, Elmer David, David Elmer—from the back porch she sounds, my father says, like a Swiss yodeler.

Brother is leaning down toward my father for some free legal advice when I see Rosie Capuccio step up to my grandmother. Rosie is dressed in pale blue. She kisses my grandmother, takes her hand. It is Rosie and not Molly B my grandmother wants for a daughter-in-law. Why? Because we all know Jimmy Doll is crazy about Rosie Capuccio and has been for six years. We all know Rosie Capuccio is crazy about my Uncle Jimmy Doll.

My uncle staggers to his feet to marry Molly B.

Why?

"Never look back," says my Uncle Ukie after the ceremony and on the way to my grandparents' house next to the river, where he knows he and his brothers will in moments be tossing back jelly glasses of tequila.

"What will be will be," says my Aunt Ella, wiping her eyes and leaning her three hundred pounds on her husband's frail arm.

"Why?" my sister and I ask when we are settled in the family car and my father is pulling out of the St. Teresa parking lot. "Why didn't Jimmy Doll marry Rosie Capuccio?"

My mother folds back the black veil from her face and pushes in the dash lighter. She needs a cigarette. We wait until she blows smoke in a soothing stream toward the narrow opening in her window.

"They agreed. They planned it. They were tired of being poor. They wanted something better. They decided together to marry somebody rich. Both of them. They agreed." Then she blows smoke out her nose and says, "Rosie's fiancé owns a laundromat."

My father starts to say something, then closes his mouth. My mother calls this keeping your own counsel. Nobody says anything until we pull up behind Pearl and Arthur's green Packard and get out of the car. My father goes on ahead, and as Mother straightens our dresses and smoothes our hair she leans in close to say, "It's just as easy to fall in love with a rich man as a poor one." Then she gives us a long look to make sure we have understood, holding us there with her eyes until at last our cousins swoop down—Arlenie, Star, Carol Dawn, Della, Terry Ann, David Elmer, Elmer David—then we all gallop off toward the front porch in a pack, whacking our hands at our sides, breathing like wild horses.

IN THE CLOSET

"You girls never play with your dolls," my mother says, sitting on my sister's bed, smoking a cigarette. She is staring into our open closet.

"We play with them all the time," says my sister, digging through a box for a cap pistol. I've already got my six shooters buckled on and a tiny knife on my belt in a sheath that says Santa Catalina Island. Becky is waiting outside for us.

"No," says my mother with feigned resignation, "you never play with them." My sister stops looking for her gun, knowing the importance of dealing with these moods when they happen. She hauls out her doll Anne by what remains of her hair. Exhibit A. Anne looks loved half to death.

Actually she is the victim of scientific experimentation. Anne has not known love. Her skin is puckered and peeling from being left out in the rain. If you shake her hard you can hear several hundred straight pins in her stomach from when we forced them through the tiny O in her mouth to see what would happen.

My sister has made a mistake, hauling out Anne. Now my mother is pulling the dolls out one by one and arranging them on the bed as if they are witnesses for the prosecution. The Dionne Quintuplets are particularly disheveled and lean for support against Raggedy Andy and Uncle Wiggly. My mother made the two stuffed dolls and that is maybe the source of her irritation. She adjusts Uncle Wiggly's waistcoat and says how there are plenty of children who would appreciate such beautiful handmade dolls. Then she brings

Cowgirls Don't Wear White Gloves. Exterior.

out those dolls with the hard bodies that are dressed up like movie stars, the ones she says will be worth a lot of money one day.

Now I do sleep with Raggedy Ann and Nurse Jane the kindly old muskrat, both made by my mother, but this does not count because of all these other abandoned dolls. My mother is having a hard time understanding how these dolls keep ending up at the back of the closet.

First, we do not like dolls that are stiff and dressed up in uncomfortable clothes that are hard to take off. Second, we do not like boy dolls. And third, who likes to play dolls anyway.

Becky likes it. She says, Let's play house. My sister and I feel sick to our stomachs whenever Becky says this. The problem is there's no story to it at all. You shop and wash dishes, feed the baby and say Hi honey on the phone. Too much like real life. A couple of guns, and a movie starts to happen all around you.

Now that the dolls are covering my sister's bed, my mother starts to look at our clothes. The ones shoved to the side where they're out of the way. Pinafores and sun dresses and velvet jumpers with straps that slip off and have to be yanked up; clothes my mother has made for us, by hand.

"You never wear these," says my mother, holding up two pinafores that look like banana cream pie. My mother has one to match; all three dresses just alike. These are Mother And Daughter outfits. My mother loves it when we are all three dressed up in them and old ladies say "My aren't you sweet you all look like sisters." We purely hate it but Mother likes it.

These dresses don't just happen. My sister and I spend hours of our time sitting on high stools in dry goods sections while Mother pages through books of patterns thick as the Los Angeles phone book or matches zippers to bolts of fabric or searches for the absolute perfect buttons.

"Sure we do," says my sister again, "we wear dresses all the time." Now she has her gun and is looking for a roll of caps.

My mother starts in on the clothes fallen onto the floor of the closet. She drags out a pair of Levis and says, "You never wear anything but pants. Pants and T-shirts and those terrible guns." I am hoping her eye is not going to fall on my baseball mitt, which is in plain sight now that she is holding up the Levis, but in the moment when I am not breathing her mood changes, softens the way light can. She turns slowly, like Bette Davis in *Dark Victory,* to gaze out the window, looking beautiful and wistful and somehow resigned.

My mother had to wear her brothers' and sisters' clothes when she was little and so now she finds it hard to see us so unappreciative for all we have. She also has a terrible aversion to boys and their wild ways, always calling them "poopy boys," as if they are not quite human, mainly because she and her three sisters had to iron their eight brothers' shirts and wait on them all the time like they were kings. Now, when she stares into our closet, she maybe has the feeling her plan to be the mother of little girls has not quite worked out the way she always thought it would.

Part of her would surely like us to put on our Mother And Daughter dresses and join her in this tranquillity and beauty. But the Ortiz y Cabares part of her believes: What will be will be. This part makes resignation and perhaps even love possible.

"Come on," says my sister, giving the chamber on her Smith and Wesson a debonair whirl. "Time to slap leather."

My mother stares in astonishment, like she has given birth to

Tom Mix and Will Rogers instead of to Shirley Temple and Elizabeth Taylor, the way she planned. "Well," she says, smoothing her hair back from her forehead and breathing in deep, "clean up your closet first."

LEGENDS

On the way to Roger Young Village my parents are arguing mildly about my Uncle Ukie and the fact that he seems perfectly happy living in a Quonset hut and could live there forever. It is two years since the war.

My father is taking the side of Uncle Ukie, to whom he is brother-in-law, and my mother is taking the side of Aunt Rosie, to whom she is no relation whatsoever. My mother takes Aunt Rosie's side because she is after all a mother and knows what it's like raising two daughters practically by herself. Here she glances sidelong and meaningfully at my father, who gives his full attention to negotiating a particularly demanding left turn, rolling down his window and signaling carefully with his left arm.

My father takes Uncle Ukie's side mostly because my mother has taken Aunt Rosie's. My father does this, waits to see which side you want and then he will take the other and happily too. He even bets this way, especially on baseball, though I have noticed he tends to lose. Never mind, he's happy just being on the other side from you.

But there is another reason my father is on Uncle Ukie's side, which is that my Uncle Ukie keeps a kite in his truck at all times so that if the wind is right he can stop and get that old kite up right then and there, wherever he is. My father, who wants a sailboat, understands this preoccupation with wind, momentum, and flight.

"He needs to face his responsibilities," my mother says, turning her face to the window.

"It's not like they're on the street," says my father.

"I remember people living in the park," I say. "They lived in boxes. There was chicken wire."

"You couldn't possibly remember that," says my father.

"Of course she does," says my mother. "Children remember things."

"She saw a newsreel."

"She remembers."

"MacArthur Park," my sister says, "when the war was over."

My mother looks at my father.

"She was older," my father says, turning into the cut-rate gas station on Riverside Drive.

"I remember gas rationing too," I say.

For awhile nobody says anything. We listen to the gas guzzling into the tank under my left arm. Then my sister says she is hungry.

"You just ate," says my mother.

When we pull into Roger Young Village and up to Aunt Rosie's and Uncle Ukie's Quonset hut, my uncle is fanning the barbecue with his Stetson hat. He is wearing Levis, the carved belt with the big silver buckle, cowboy boots, and a faded army shirt. His hair is all crinkly brown, waving back from his forehead, and his eyes look Chinese. He walks over to the car with his arms out, ready to grab everybody. My cousins Star and Carol Dawn run over from next door. Kids are everywhere. When we come here we run in packs, like dogs, my mother says.

Aunt Rosie comes out with potato salad and Uncle Ukie puts ribs on the grill. He wraps up ears of corn in foil and throws them onto the charcoal. Star and Carol Dawn and my sister and I all run around like wild things while our parents sit at the picnic table and talk next to the cooking ribs. Finally they call us.

While I am holding my plate for Uncle Ukie to serve me with his big fork I suddenly remember what Mother told me, about the time when she was a girl and got up one morning hearing voices in the kitchen. When she opened the door, there was Uncle Ukie standing at the stove flipping pancakes for three tramps. Telling them stories too. Years later they found a little mark on their fence post, made by tramps. It said in secret tramp code: These people will feed you and tell you stories. One little mark meant all this.

I take my heavy plate, sit between Star and Carol Dawn. My uncle named them, lying in a foxhole one night. Star has dark curly, curly hair like her daddy and Carol Dawn has straight light hair like her mother, but they both got the Chinese eyes all right. I honestly don't think they mind about the Quonset hut. Once I spent the night with Star and Carol Dawn, and the people on the other end of the Quonset hut had their bedroom right up against our beds. We could hear them talk through the wall. It did not feel like going to bed alone.

It takes me a long time to eat the corn on account of my front teeth. But the grown-ups keep talking and the neighborhood kids who have been running around like chickens with their heads cut off go inside for their dinner and the afternoon light softens around us. My uncle is talking about going to Mexico. My father is listening intently because one day he wants to retire and take the whole family to live there. My uncle is telling what he will take in his truck on this trip, besides the kite. He has done this before, and nobody goes with him.

First, he takes a dozen little leather pouches with jacks in them. Yes, jacks like we play with. In fact, my uncle is the person who taught me to play jacks. If you can play jacks, he thinks, then you can do anything. He takes these jacks with him to some little village that is special to him, and invites the mayor to play. The mayor never knows how. They sit cross-legged on the floor of my uncle's hotel room and play jacks over and over until the mayor understands. Then my uncle gives the bag of jacks to the mayor as a gift. The next day he plays with a different man, and the next a different one, each time sending the man away with his own set of jacks in a little leather bag.

For the children he brings pencils. It is important to have pencils and the children in Mexico are too poor, so my uncle saves pencils all year and gets all the people at Lockheed to save them. Like when they get half used up, don't throw them away because someone would really like that pencil. Give them to old Uke the Duke, he tells them. So when he is ready for his trip he has hundreds of pencils.

He drives into the village. The children see him from a great distance. Dust rises in clouds from the wheels of his American truck. The Man with the Silver Buckle, they shout. The Man with the Silver Buckle is coming. They run behind his truck as he enters the village. At the plaza he stops and gets out. They know exactly what he brings them, the prize above all others. He stands there, my uncle, his great hands enclosing the two hundred pencils. They wait, breathless. Into the sparkling air The Man with the Silver Buckle tosses the two hundred pencils; up, up, up, up and arcing, spraying down like rain, children scrambling, their fingers closing around their own pencil, the one he has brought them.

"Well," says my mother, "Rosie might like to go to Las Vegas with you instead."

Las Vegas is where my family talks about going. Vegas. My mother and Aunt Thelma like to play the slots. My Uncle Earl plays the ponies. He loses at the races what my aunt wins at the slots. My Aunt Thelma is so good at slot machines she has to carry her money around in buckets. She was a bookie herself once and got arrested for it. She met interesting people in the Lincoln Heights jail and they sat up all night telling stories. But when my Aunt Thelma says to my Uncle Roonie, "Let's all go to Las Vegas," she means he might want to think about getting married to Mickie instead of just living with her forever, as he is inclined to do. "Let's all go to Las Vegas," she says, when she is feeling frisky and devilish, or just wants to see his face turn pale as the moon.

Aunt Rosie is looking like she might want to say something on the topic of Las Vegas, but suddenly my father and Uncle Ukie jump up from the table because my uncle wants Star to show everybody how well she can shoot her bow and arrow. On the other side of the Quonset hut bales of hay are stacked up with a target stuck onto them. Star has a real bow. She strings it herself, snugging it against her left foot then bending her weight over it perfectly until she can slip the string easily up onto the notch. She slings a bag of arrows on her back. Star is just my age. She fits the notched end of the arrow onto the string and pulls back, steady and strong. The air twangs and the arrow strikes almost exactly next to the bull's eye. She lets me try and the first time I thump the soft inside of my arm hard with the string and the second time

I slice across my hand with the sharp feathers, but it is dark enough that I am the only one who knows.

That's what I think until going up the front stairs to the house Uncle Ukie leans close and says into my ear, "Don't lose your skate key, kid."

Inside Aunt Rosie has turned on some lamps and she and Mother are drinking coffee and smoking cigarettes and laughing. They make room on the couch for Uncle Ukie and my father. In the kids' room we get out the Monopoly game, and as my sister counts out four stacks of money, I get down on the braided rug next to my cousins and just lie there, feeling lazy and dreamy, listening with them to the murmuring through the walls.

My father is standing behind my chair, his hands on my hands as we allow the pressure of the steak knife to do its job. There is no need, my father explains, returning to his place at the head of the table, ever to exert pressure. Cutting meat is a question of control and weight, measure and balance. A person who knows the correct way to cut meat will never struggle.

I look at his mustache. There is a tiny crest of parsley resting just under his left nostril. I study my meat. If I lift my eyes from

DINNER 1947

my plate, my sister's eyes will find mine. One of us will surely laugh.

My sister reaches for the milk pitcher. She is in dangerous territory. The pitcher may have been a little closer to Mother than to her. This miscalculation, together with the fact of the parsley just under my father's left nostril, has thrown her balance a little off. The milk brims up and over the rim of the glass, puddling onto the tablecloth. Mother and Daddy leap up at exactly the same moment and begin folding the tablecloth toward the center, like a flag. Nobody has said a word.

When they are settled back down in their places and our plates are resting on clean woven place mats, my father clears his throat and says in a calm tone, "Tomorrow, Hanny, I want you to take a glass and a pitcher of water outside and practice pouring." My sister does not look up. She hates to be called Hanny.

My mother is cutting her meat, exerting a little pressure, just on the verge of struggling. My father clears his throat. The parsley is still there. I try looking just past him, at the wall behind. The wall is painted blue up to my waist, then white, like a Mexican house. On the wall just to the side of my father's left ear hangs Pancho Villa's whip.

My mother has told me the story. Pancho Villa and his men

riding up to the family's ranch house. Pancho Villa leaning down from his saddle. My mother scooped up in his right arm and held inside the sweet odor of sweat and trail. Pancho Villa arriving or leaving, she is not sure which. But amidst embracing and shouted greetings. And when Pancho Villa sets down my mother he lifts a long coiled whip of braided leather from his saddle horn and hands it to my grandfather, who accepts it in all honor. There it hangs on the wall just to the side of my father's left ear.

I cut my meat slowly and carefully, under my father's eye. The meat is tough. I chew, counting. Everything needs to be chewed a hundred times.

My sister raises her napkin as if to wipe her mouth and spits into it the impossible meat. Then she looks at the whip on the wall behind my father, lowers the napkin to her lap. She is remembering the other story of Pancho Villa's whip, the time when the whip still hung on the wall of my grandmother's house by the river and my Uncle Jimmy Doll came home from school, her youngest, beaten by the principal, crying.

My grandmother took that whip down from the wall, carried it coiled in her hand, walking all the way to Allesandro Street School, the school built on the land of her own people, carried that whip into the main office, called out the principal, whipped him as he had whipped her son.

My sister is feeling now my grandmother's brown hands on hers, the weight of her strong hands guiding her own, showing her the simple balance of justice.

RIVERSIDE DRIVE

I am hanging by my knees from the monkey bars at Allesandro Street school, waiting for my sister, who is in Mrs. Schubert's fifth grade and gets out an hour later than me. She is lucky to be in Mrs. Schubert's because of the bees. In Mrs. Schubert's classroom is an entire hive enclosed in glass. Everything they learn is by the bees. Long division, everything. When I am in fifth grade I will have Mrs. Schubert and the bees myself.

Once I went in to find my sister, after school was out. She was finishing a test. There was a humming in the room. Mrs. Schubert got up from her big desk to show me the bees like she was introducing her family. There must have been thousands of them, all streaming up and down the glass tube that hooked them to the window, or climbing over each other inside the hive. Mrs. Schubert explained how it was a whole organized world. A society, she kept saying, blinking her honey-colored eyelashes.

They all have jobs, except the drones, who don't do much at all, except when the queen needs to make more babies. Then they all fly up, up, up, until the queen chooses one to help her. Then the queen gets busy. She lays hundreds and hundreds of eggs, and the nursery bees feed them and raise them up. The bees coming and going through the tubes are getting the pollen for the honey and making very special little pots of something called Royal Jelly to feed only to the queen.

Oh, they all have something to do and the honey is not their only thing, but I was glad when Mrs. Schubert gave me a little bit of the honey comb, so sweet and crunchy, not like you'd expect. After that I sat down in a desk, waiting, listening to the drowsy bees, listening to my sister's big green pencil moving across thick paper.

She appears now, upside down.

"Come on," she says. One of her pigtails is undone. No ribbon. The other ribbon is almost off.

I drop down beside her.

"It's in my pocket," she says.

We go to the girl's bathroom. Nobody is there except two girls from Mrs. Schubert's class scrubbing off their lipstick before they go home. I unbraid my sister's fine hair and comb it with my fingers, watching out of the corner of my eye the girls plopping pine soap onto coarse brown paper towels and scrubbing their soft lips clean. I gather my sister's hair into equal strands and braid it carefully back, as nearly like my mother's braiding as I can. The girls are rinsing their swollen lips. I tie the red ribbons onto the two pigtails, trying to make the wrinkles in the ribbons come out in the same places.

Every day before we walk home we do this, trying to make my sister's slippery hair look like it has not moved all day. Otherwise she will be in trouble. But today we are not going home. Instead we will walk the other way, toward the river, and stay at my grandmother's house for the afternoon.

On the days when we walk home, there are the Red Car tracks to step over carefully with those electrical wires snapping overhead. When we go to my grandmother's, there is Riverside Drive to cross. We can hear it before we smell it. Riverside Drive, sound in waves breaking off the speeding cars and washing up on the school steps. My heart pounds. I look at my sister's pigtails, then into her dark brown eyes. Both hold steady. She takes my hand.

We start down. The two girls from the bathroom pass us, laughing, running toward the traffic. They stand at the curb, their skirts lifted by waves of air from hot tires. A car honks. They grab hands and dart across the wide boulevard, dodging cars like bull fighters.

We are never to do this. Always, my father has said, use the underpass.

But the underpass is dark and long. We start down the staircase, still holding hands. My free hand trails the bannister, catches on something sticky. An acrid smell grows the deeper down we go, a smell like cat pee. The way levels out ahead, but there is no natural light, only a dim electric glow from overhead lights surrounded by gasoline haze.

Behind me I hear a slapping sound, a sound like when my sister is being spanked. It gets closer—the slap, slap, slap. And then a boy careens past us, the slap, slap, slap growing distant. We must be halfway, maybe more. Overhead the cars mumble like provoked bees.

My sister squeezes my hand. "Don't look," she says. A man in the dimness ahead, his back toward us, leans against the wall, fumbles with his fly. I look away, hear a stream of water hit the wall, smell hot ammonia. "Run," she whispers fiercely.

All the races we have ever run, barefoot down dirt roads, have prepared us for this. We bolt forward like race horses, braids flying, until we are well beyond him, our steps echoing, the light growing stronger, as we take the stairs two at a time, then lean panting on the railing, next to the river of traffic.

Book Two

STREET MAP

1620 FARGO STREET

She is going to take her time about this. She will not be hurried. Winifred sits down at her dressing table, ties the silk flowered kimono more securely, smoothes it across her breasts. She is fragrant from her bath. The skirt from the dressing table folds about her knees: flowered chintz. She is artistic. Robert has told her this. Only Robert has known her. She picks up the polish remover, a cotton ball. The bedroom door flies open.

"You going to be ready any time soon?" says this other.

"Make me a highball," she tells the other. She feels him waiting. He might do anything. Hit her even.

She unscrews the cap from the polish remover. Looks at him. "Well?"

He turns in the doorway. He casts shadows wherever he goes. Inside this house that she hates. On this street that she hates. He has left the door open. They are eating up her space again, leaving her no air to breathe. "You come here," she yells at him, "and close this goddamn door." In the silence she waits. The sharp sound of ice trays; nothing else.

Where are they, then, she wonders, beginning to remove the old polish, those two? Creeping around the house holding hands, judging her, who was after all their mother. She tosses the used-up cotton into the trash, takes up another; then suddenly she rises, leans across the foot of the bed, swings the door shut fiercely.

Now that she is up, she stands, staring at the bed she can no longer sleep in.

Robert says she is too finely made.

She sees his pale hands gathering the drapes in folds, the way he stood that day, stepping back like an artist to see if they hung just so.

Artsy fartsy, Ted had said when he was gone, when he still stood leaning out the window, watching Robert's sky blue van inching slowly up Fargo and out of sight. Could have got drapes from god-damn Sears but no she had to have custom made.

She weaves her fingers into the folds of the kimono at her neck, is standing so when this other abruptly opens the door, holds the rum and coke out to her. Holds it across the bed.

"Have they called?" she asks, taking the drink, sitting down again at the dressing table, smoothing her kimono. She sips, folds a kleenex, sets the glass on top.

"Thelma," he says, sitting on the bed.

She looks at him in the mirror. His legs are spread. He is fat, off center in the softness. Little crescents of fat ride under his eyes making him look Chinese. Robert is slender, wears black slacks, dress shirts, silk ties. Ted's cowboy shirt is open at the throat; his undershirt shows at the neck. She works on her thumb, removing the last of the polish. "What are the kids doing?"

"I dressed 'em," he says.

"They better not be getting dirty," she says, putting on foundation. "Christmas or no Christmas."

"What do you care," says her husband.

"They're a reflection," she says.

He looks at her. She is penciling on eyebrows.

"Beats the hell out of me."

"What beats the hell out of you?"

"You really want to know?" he asks. "If they're a reflection then why'd you chop her hair all funny like that? I can't even comb it, time you were done with her."

The phone rings.

"That's them again," he says, stirring to get up.

"Let it ring," she says. "Thelma knows I'm trying to get ready. I don't know why she can't give it a rest."

"They're waiting," he says.

She picks up a lipstick. It's the wrong one. "Damn," she says. Searches among the tubes.

"You've got one hell of a mouth," he says, "for a lady."

"A lot you know." She leans forward, draws two sides of a bow on her mouth, extends the line out with a brush.

He has finished his drink, gives a Chinese squint. "You done?" he asks.

"I told you I'm not ready yet."

"Drink, I mean." He rattles his ice cubes in explanation.

She looks at the sweaty glass. The color dims toward the surface, like a sunset. "You could freshen it," she says.

She never knows what he will do. Now he is standing over her, his face gone purple. "Freshen my ass," he is shouting. Two pale faces appear momentarily in the doorway, then disappear. "Wait in the car!" he yells in their direction.

It is coming now, and she had wanted just stillness, this time of her own. She had wanted to control the waiting and the time and it was slipping out of her hands, getting away from her.

"Ted, honey," she says.

"Freshen, my ass. Why can't you just answer a simple question. For once." He is pacing now, back and forth, as if the matter of answering a simple question has been oppressing him all his life. "For once." His gestures have become exaggerated, imploring. "Just this once." Now his balled fist is smacking into his left hand, making a sound as familiar as her heart.

2710 ALLESANDRO STREET

"I don't know," says my Aunt Thelma, hanging up the phone, "what could be keeping them."

I am sticking toothpicks into Mypapa's backgammon board shaped into a Chinese serpent. But I am listening too. Listening and waiting, here with all of my aunts and uncles and cousins, waiting in the warm house for presents to happen. But not until Uncle Ted and Aunt Winifred get here, the grown-ups say.

They don't live far. Only on Fargo Street. I've been there. They live on the steepest street in L.A. When you go there you think your car will just fall off backwards. Inside their house you feel that way too. Then later, when you leave, at the top of the hill you can't see anything, just space all around, until finally the hood of your car tips down and you can see where you are.

"That Winifred," says my mother.

"I just feel sorry for the children," says my Aunt Thelma, who has no children and would like some to spoil. "Especially that precious Terry Ann."

"Her hair," says my mother, shaking her head, absently stroking my hair.

"I don't know why God gives children to people who don't even deserve them, let alone want them," says my Aunt Thelma.

"Well, he won't be giving them any more," says my Uncle Earl with a yelp of laughter.

My mother and his wife look at him. He is not of their family, only married to my Aunt Thelma.

"That's right," says my Uncle Earl, "he got himself fixed after the last one."

"Fixed?" I say.

"Earl Fox!" say my aunt and my mother together.

1610 FARGO STREET

He is looking at his wife in the mirror. Her top lip is bright and red with lipstick. But the bottom lip remains invisible, undefined. She is looking at him. Waiting. He feels the blood leaving his muscles. It is Christmas. His whole family is waiting on the other side of Elysian Park. "Let's go," he says.

"I'm not ready," she says. "But almost."

The telephone rings.

"It's them," he calls from the next room.

2710 ALLESANDRO STREET

My cousins and I are sitting around Mymama and Mypapa's tree watching colored oil bubbling in glass candles. We are waiting.

There is a humming behind us where the grown-ups stand. There is a story back there. The story is the one not being told to the children. The grown-ups tell the story to each other, in whispers. The children watch the bubbling tree lights, listening intently to the story not being told.

1610 FARGO STREET

Winifred sits at her dressing table, having gathered time back into her hands like escaped fabric. Ted and the children are going to wait in the car until she is ready. The blank paper is in front of her. She has etched in her bottom lip. Her face is on. With her eyebrow pencil she writes across the empty sheet of paper, "I am pregnant." Then she waits, as if something more will come to her. Eventually she puts down the pencil, slides the paper away from her.

Ted's gun in her hand feels cool. She curves her fingers over the muzzle as if warming it, observes in the mirror this artistic woman whose art is in her face. Then she pulls aside the kimono, rests the muzzle against her breast, and pulls the trigger.

2710 ALLESANDRO STREET

The front door swings open. Warm air and light rush out of the house and curve around the three people standing in the brightening doorway: blank-faced Uncle Ted gripping his small son's shoulder with one big hand and with the other holding his baby girl tight against his cowboy shirt.

We are all watching from beneath the tree, cousins, not breathing, still as ornaments. My Aunt Thelma steps toward the three as deliberately as if she is in a Christmas play, and having heard at long last her cue, reaches forth empty arms to receive her long-delayed daughter.

Winifred, Her Story. Exterior.

THE BIRTHDAY PARTY

I breathe in the fragrant burning wax from Karen Halverson's birthday candles. Her father holds a lighter over the seventh candle. We all bend toward the flickering candles to study the art of Karen Halverson's birthday cake. This is no ordinary cake. This one is store bought. Even Becky's mother, who records birthdays with an eight millimeter camera, makes her own cakes and usually her own ice cream. In Becky's front lawn is a permanent circle of brown where we take turns cranking the handle on the ice cream mixer. Karen Halverson's birthday party suggests a world beyond family and neighborhood.

I gaze into the cake, a sheet cake decorated to look like the swimming pool the Halverson's will build next summer. Pink children swim in blue-green frosting. We lift our voices in song. Mrs. Halverson fires off little bulbs from her camera. I am happy, at my first real birthday party. I have come here without my big sister. I stand singing between Hazel Medina and Terry Taylor, my mouth tasting of burning candles and crepe paper. Karen Halverson blows at the candles. Terry Taylor squeezes my hand.

Terry Taylor is pale and blond and thin. My mother likes him because he has been raised by his grandmother. Terry Taylor looks a little bit like my white rat at home in its wood cage smelling of moist fur and shredded newspaper, though Terry Taylor is always clean and ironed because of his grandmother. I have decided to marry Terry Taylor eventually so that I won't ever have to change my name. But it is Hazel Medina, with her dark, dark eyes smoldering like extinguished candles, Hazel I love. Oh Hazel. I squeeze her hand as Mrs. Halverson plunges the ice cream scoop into half a gallon of Ralph's grocery store vanilla. Karen holds a big kitchen knife by herself. She runs the knife the length of the cake. The pink skin of the swimmers streaks and reddens in the water, as if sharks have attacked. I look into Karen's face but she is thinking of presents.

We sit down at the long table. The fragrant crepe paper table-cloth blossoms around me, fills my lap. I press it back, take a pink paper plate from Mrs. Halverson. Cake and ice cream. Neither one smelling like any birthday before this one. I pick up my fork. Terry Taylor suddenly pushes his plate back against his cup of nuts and candy and his popper. He might throw up. Hazel has a smear of frosting below her nose like a little pink moustache. The ice cream tastes faintly of machines. I lick my lip, look sideways at Hazel. We laugh. Mrs. Halverson brings Terry Taylor a glass of water but he does not drink it. Then it is time to open presents.

Karen gets two plastic purses just alike. When she picks up my present, she says, "Oh, a book," without even opening it. She is sitting in a nest of crushed wrapping paper, reaching for the next present.

I suddenly feel tired. I am only two blocks from Mymama's house, but it feels like two thousand miles. Terry Taylor is lying back in the wrapping paper, his face like white tissue paper. Hazel Medina brought a card but no present. She is looking out the window the way she does at school when she is thinking of home.

Mrs. Halverson knows it's time to play games. First we drop clothes pins into a bottle. Joyce Alsace wins a play watch that Louis Wheeler grabs and breaks. Mrs. Halverson says maybe Louis needs his own prize so she gives him a detective badge. Next we play

Pin the Tail on the Donkey. Mrs. Halverson takes a picture of the birthday girl pinning a tail on the startled cat and then we all get to go outside.

We stand a little stunned near the front door, on a grassy hill that slopes down toward a white picket fence and the sidewalk beyond. Then Louis Wheeler sets off his popper and the girls all scream but keep their place in the circle. In the moment when we are all waiting for the next thing to happen, a breeze moves through the stillness and suddenly my Uncle Ovaldo comes into view.

He is moving slowly along Karen Halverson's white picket fence. His old brown hat is pulled down low over his deep eyes. Grey hair kinks out on either side. He looks small down there. His house slippers make a whispering sound on the sidewalk. He is moving methodically, like a duck in a shooting gallery. He looks like he will whirl around and go back to his little house where geraniums bloom out of old cars in the front yard, back where he came from, when he reaches the end of Karen Halverson's fence.

"That's my Uncle O.V.," I say.

To my astonishment, they laugh.

"No really," I say.

They laugh again. Not Terry Taylor and Hazel Medina. But Karen Halverson laughs. And Louis Wheeler. And Joyce Alsace. And Eleanor Manning. Like I am telling a joke.

And when they laugh this second time I break from them, running like a wild thing down the hill toward this dark man I know is really my uncle. By now I am panting, pleading with him, "Uncle O.V. Ovaldo, mi tío." But he can't hear me. He keeps moving under the pulled-down hat, in his own world the way Mymama always says, and at the end of the fence he does not turn but keeps on, and keeps on, his house slippers saying shush, shush, shush.

My father, my sister, and I sit at the table waiting for my mother
to get the butter out of the refrigerator. She is in the kitchen.
We are in the dining room. My father leans forward in his chair
and whispers, "The biscuits are like hockey pucks."

Neither of us knows what a hockey puck is.

When my mother sits down, my father says amiably,
"Honey, these biscuits are a little tough."

D I N N E R   1 9 4 8

My mother says nothing, passes
the butter.

There is a strange field of energy emanating from my father.
His dark eyes have a glitter to them. Something to do with the
biscuits.

When the butter reaches me I smear some on, bring the
biscuit to my mouth. The top is warm and soft, flour brushes my
upper lip. I lick. Good. The bottom is hard and crunchy. It tastes
a little like the charcoal briquettes Becky and I ate out of her
barbecue grill one day when her mother was downtown, only
better. Jam helps. I eat my eggs. I like breakfast for dinner. I knock
my knife off the plate and everybody looks at me.

My mother gets up with her plate. Most of her dinner is still
there. My sister sits, trying not to knock over her milk. My father's
eyes still have that glittery look to them.

"Come on," he says, getting up suddenly. He picks up the
basket of biscuits. "Let's go outside."

It's a funny time to go outside. He hands the basket to my
sister. We follow him out the kitchen door and along the path
that circles behind the house.

It is winter and dark, except for the moon. We jump off the
stone retaining wall one by one, like paratroopers on a mission.
I can tell now we're going to the high tension tower, that skeletal
structure that looms next to our house, the one all the mothers

say to stay off of, that a boy, they say, climbed too high, they say, and electrocuted himself.

I know how he did it, touching one of those giant electrical pine cones way up at the very, very top. He must have reached out, as if for a flower. I see him sometimes in my dreams, outlined in blue fire.

That's why whenever Becky and I climb up the tower we are careful not to go very high, shinnying up only to the first level, then walking carefully around like tightrope walkers.

Suddenly my father stops at the foot of the tower, my sister bumping into him, and I into her. We wait, listening. There is only the sound of crickets, the smell of electrical energy. High tension.

My father takes a biscuit, tosses it lightly in the air, catches it, then winds up and hurls it full force at the tower. A metallic twang comes back at him. Has he laughed? I don't know. He puts a biscuit in my hand. One in my sister's. A second biscuit careens through the night, leaving a hand, but whose? And then the sound, the continuing and repeated sound the electrocuted boy must have made when he fell like a burning torch through the night, betrayed by height and distance and time.

HOLY LAND

We feel like we're flying. Here we are on our two wheelers racing down one hill and halfway up the next, peddling like mad to the top, and then flying down the next. We are on our way to the Holy Land. It's Sunday. Daddy is at the studio rehearsing for "Our Miss Brooks" and Mother went to take Aunt Frances and Aunt Maggie a pineapple upside down cake.

Nobody knows we come here: to the Holy Land. Once Mother found ticket stubs in my sister's pocket when she was doing the laundry. We said Oh, that's from the movies last week. But it was really the Holy Land and we pay our own way here.

We're lucky to have this special place practically in our own neighborhood. Outside, of course, it doesn't look like much. We park our bikes thinking about what's inside. There's a little brass bell that says, Please Ring. We do, and the quiet man opens the door. He knows us, I guess, but he never says much because he is a missionary and has a lot on his mind. He takes our fifty-cent pieces and hands us ticket stubs torn in half. We put them in our pockets, thinking we will have to get rid of them later.

A picture of him is right there on the wall in the first room. He stands next to his wife and they are both dressed in safari clothes, but no guns. Lots of children wearing not much at all stand around both of them, waiting like they are just about to get presents. In the background is a small airplane only big enough for two people. Under the photograph a little printed sign says, "Rev. Settles and his wife in the Holy Land." All the photographs in the first room have little signs explaining, but this is not our favorite room. Our favorite is the last, but we try not to rush through everything because of the fifty cents each.

The next room has old broken pots and bones and strange coins and dusty books lying open, but all inside glass to keep your fingers off. Everything smells like dust and earthworms, and instead of doors there are bead curtains so that every time the Reverend Settles or his wife goes in or comes out there is a gentle ticking of the beads against each other, almost like my grandmother's rosary. It is cool and a little dark in here, almost as if we are under ground and the sound of the Settles coming and going so quietly, putting little signs on everything, feels like going to sleep only safer.

Finally we get to the third room, the one we have been waiting for. In the middle is an old wooden box shaped like a body and inside is the mummy. Little signs tell about how old the mummy is and not to touch it because extreme antiquity makes it fragile and all. We go close as the velvet ropes let us, stand quietly, breathing.

The person inside must look like butterfly wings. We know we will have to save up so we can come again and see this.

Outside we blink in the light like bandages have been taken off our eyes. The way back is slower.

LA FRONTERA

"Ay dos mío," exclaims my mother, slicing into her left index finger with her paring knife.

My father is at the top of his stepladder, changing the kitchen light bulb, not realizing he is wearing his sunglasses and there is nothing wrong with the bulb. Now he is arrested in his movement both by my mother's cry of pain and by her mispronunciation of *dios*. He descends, wraps her finger in his clean and ironed hanky, and steers her gently in the direction of the dining room where he keeps his Spanish books for just such emergencies.

None of my aunts and uncles can speak Spanish and don't want to, a fact which my father finds regrettable. They have a few phrases—like "Ay dos mío" or my Uncle Ukie's favorite "That's a lot of cangada"—but my father is the only one who can speak Spanish with Mymama or Aunt Frances or Aunt Maggie or Uncle Ovaldo. My father tells my mother they are losing their own Mexican heritage. Whenever he says this her eyes get black as olives and she says, "We're not Mexicans, we're Early Californians."

Nevertheless my mother is now sitting at her own dining room table with her finger wrapped in my father's handkerchief and a first-year Spanish textbook open before her at lesson three. This book is called optimistically enough, *Hablamos Español, We Speak Spanish*. They have been on lesson three for more than six months. My mother will read along fine the first three or four sentences but it's like a road where the bridge has washed out and never gets repaired. The problem sentence is, "*Hay dos personas . . .*" Whenever my mother gets to this place on the road toward the mastery of the Spanish language, she says the English word *hay* (like for horses).

My father thinks of himself as having infinite patience and a certain talent for teaching difficult concepts through clever ways of remembering things. In this case he says, "That ain't hay." Well, actually he tends to shout it. Afterward he is sorry and embarrassed, though he does not ever get over expecting to teach my mother Spanish.

So today after he yells "That ain't hay," partly as an act of contrition and partly as a pedagogical exercise, he loads us all up in the car for a visit to Aunt Frances and Aunt Maggie. Actually it's a visit to Uncle Jake too, but Uncle Jake just sits all day on the front porch, his head trembling ever so slightly, like Mr. Nimms's cocker spaniel after it got distemper.

When we pull up, there he is, sitting in his rocker wearing his suit. My father always greets him heartily, as if by saying "Hi, Uncle Jake" with enough energy some will pass into this old man. It never does.

Uncle Jake used to work for the railroad and still always carries his Southern Pacific watch in his vest pocket. He's married to Aunt Frances but Aunt Maggie never married anybody and so lives with them in this neat little white frame house in Chavez Ravine, not far from Mymama, who is their sister. My mother kisses Uncle Jake, and by now Aunt Frances and Aunt Maggie have flung open the front door.

Aunt Frances looks like one of the quick birds that frequent her own garden. She is small and dark with sparkling eyes and cool hands. She hugs me and calls me "the little teacher" and I try again telling her I'm not going to be one but she always smiles and seems not to hear. A teacher herself, she is retired now and in charge of the beautiful garden that grows all around their neat white frame house. Also, she does the cooking. It is said Aunt Maggie cannot boil water, but she does keep the house unbelievably neat and shining.

Doilies everywhere, and gleaming wood floors and the furniture all polished. Aunt Maggie is thick and solid in the waist and smells of face powder. She always says, "Oh honey girl," and pulls you close. Then she holds you off and peers into your eyes, her own dark ones shining at you from out of the starkest white powder you ever saw. But because her own face is so brown there is a circle of natural around each eye that sets it off strangely, making her look like a kind owl, staring curiously.

My father starts talking to Aunt Maggie in Spanish and Aunt Frances hurries off into the kitchen to make coffee. My sister and I wander over to the table of family pictures, a forest of silver frames covering a large round table. In the center are my great grandmother Teresa Cabares and my great grandfather Miguel Ortiz. All around them are smaller photographs of their children, whom we name off silently: Mymama, Gullape, Julia, Frances, Madeline, Margarita, Florencio, and Ovaldo.

In one of the photographs my great grandparents stand together stiffly, he holding his hat. He is old enough to be her father, which my mother says is how things were done then.

In another photograph my great grandmother stands alone and in that one you can see it, that she must really have been an Indian princess and not an Early Californian at all. Aunt Frances always lifts her chin and says, "She was over six feet tall." My sister and I stare and stare at this, our favorite photograph.

Then it is time for cookies. My mother carries in the coffee pot, Aunt Frances the china cups. Aunt Maggie sits on the horse-hair couch with my father, talking about the old days when they lived at Lake Elizabeth, and when she politely shifts into English because my mother has sat down across from her, she still lisps it, "Elithabeth," she says, as if caressing the past.

Aunt Frances brings glasses of milk to my sister and me, then sits down next to my mother. They look alike. Identical noses and beautiful cheeks. The same smile. The same angle of looking. Now Aunt Frances notices the band aid on my mother's finger and holds her hand, patting it, as if she is her mother.

My own mother has told me this story, the story of the day Aunt Frances arrived at her sister Della's house, the house of My-mama, to ask a favor. "You have so many children," she said to her sister. "And I have none. Give me Juanita. She can have her own room, and sometimes a new dress from the Sears and Roebuck."

There was silence in the little house. My grandmother breathed in. "It is true I have many children," she said.

"Thirteen," reminded my aunt.

"Yes," agreed my grandmother. Her eye must have wandered over to Juanita, observed the dress made of a flour sack ("At least it's clean," she always told them), marked the tense beautiful face about to blossom into what even she could not guess. "But I do not have too many."

"But she looks like me," objected my Aunt Frances.

My mother sat quietly, in her disappointment and in her relief.

She passes the cookies now to her aunt. Their lovely, brown flower faces shine in their pleasure at one another, while Aunt Maggie, in white face, beams. She hands me the cookies next, says, "Oh honey girl."

Later we stand on their small porch, kissing and hugging. My father is shaking Uncle Jake's thin hand and shouting at him a little. Aunt Frances reaches into the hibiscus at the railing, breaks off a twig, and hands it to my mother. "Here, honey, put this in water," she tells her. "It will grow."

CURANDERA

My sister dips a carmine red pencil into the glass of water at her elbow and twirls it. A thin spiral of color hangs suspended momentarily, then turns the water pink. We are lying on our stomachs listening to "Grand Central Station" on Sunday radio. My sister applies the wet colored pencil to the left nostril of the palomino horse rearing up on her thick sketch pad. My sister is an artist. She can paint or draw anything, especially horses. Dogs too. All over the floor are the tools of her trade: soft pencils, art gum erasers, scissors, glue, charcoal sticks, tubes of paint. My father calls this scissors and paste, especially when he can't walk through it.

Into the pert ear of the stallion my sister inserts a purple arc. My mother explains this is how she must see it. The ear might not be purple to everyday people, but it is to my sister, and that is art. My mother understands this because of her time painting yo-yos.

Not since kindergarten when Eleanor Manning objected to my floating calcimine sky have I felt comfortable as anything but an appreciative patron of the arts. I roll over on my back and try to follow the convoluted narrative line of *Grand Central Station,* "crossroads of a million private lives."

"There's a new art teacher," says my sister, shattering my tenuous grasp on the intricate and invisible character relationships. My sister is in her last semester at Allesandro Street School and is probably being readied for her career in junior high next fall. But no, she explains, everybody is going to have the new art teacher. Everybody.

It's Thursday before I actually *do* have her. But I have already heard she is not just an art teacher, but a counselor too. "What's a counselor?" I ask my friend Ann. Ann is the janitor and has an office that used to be a closet. There's just enough room in there for Ann's desk and chair, and a second chair pulled up close, which is where I sit when I come to visit at recess. Ann has a warm piney smell to her and a voice like honey. She is going over some kind of check list and making little marks with a big green school pencil. "I think that's where they took my Aunt Pearl when she talked to her Chihuahuas."

"They taking you there, sugar?" she asks me, looking up.

"They took Pig Nose already," I say. "Just called her out of class."

"Well Pig Nose, yes." She goes back to checking.

That afternoon Mrs. Beardsley lines the whole fourth grade up by the door, two by two. We walk outside toward the temporary building holding hands. Hazel Medina is my partner. A soft breeze lifts her bangs. She catches me smiling at her. When we get to the art teacher's room giant pieces of fresh paper are waiting for us all and paint boxes that no one has ever used before.

The teacher is short and square, looks like a gingerbread boy with glistening raisin eyes. She has on a blue artist's smock and thick shoes that look like they are made out of art gum erasers and make no noise at all. Her hair looks like it was cut with a bowl; black hair but with wisps of gray rising from each temple like little wings. When Eleanor Manning asks her what we should paint, Mrs. Van Prague says, "Whatever you like, dears."

I paint like crazy all period. I paint the stories in my head. Eleanor, looking over my shoulder says, "That's not right."

The next day a messenger comes to Mrs. Beardsley's class and hands a note saying Jeanene Chaney and I are supposed to go to

Mrs. Van Prague's room. Jeanene carries the big wooden hall pass that says "Mrs. Beardsley." We walk slowly down the hall. Ann is pushing green sawdust along with her wide broom. She looks at me and rolls her eyes. "They done sent for you," she says. Then Jeanene, who never says much of anything to anybody, hands me the wooden hall pass and starts walking across the play yard toward her house, which is only two blocks away.

Ann and I stand watching until Jeanene disappears. "You go on ahead now. You be fine," says Ann.

Mrs. Van Prague's door is standing open. She's working on the blackboard, covering it with brightly colored chalk shapes that make it look like a stained glass window. "Oh, hi," she says, leaning back on one of the desks, half sitting, breathing as if she has just walked up stairs or something.

"Jeanene couldn't come," I say. "She had to go home."

"Oh, I'm sorry about that," she says, "because I wanted you both to do something for me. Something special."

Unaccountably I feel like crying. I don't know whether I'm talking to the art teacher or the counselor.

"Listen," she says, taking my hand and leading me to a chair and squatting down on her thick black shoes to be eye level with me, "is anybody in your family a storyteller?"

I study her raisin eyes. I start running through my family beginning with my Aunt Thelma and ending with my uncle Uke the Duke. I nod.

"Well, I thought so. This is what I want you to do. I want you to tell stories to the first and second graders every couple of weeks. Paint pictures to go with them."

"You mean stand up in front of everybody and talk?"

"As a favor to me," she says.

I feel confused. I see Jeanene walking alone toward the gate, leaving this. Running film backwards, I see myself sitting and chatting in Ann's office or hanging on the fence talking to Hazel Medina all those days instead of leaping into the center of the dodgeball game, where Mr. Ruffino blows the whistle and smacks the ball against his open palm.

"My mother always hated school," I tell her. "My Aunt Thelma hated it too. My Aunt Thelma says every morning when she wakes up she *still* says to herself, 'Thelma, you don't have to go to school today.' I'm probably going to be just like that."

"This is not what you think," she says. I am not sure what she thought I thought it was, or even what I *did* think it was. My eyes are swimming in misery. She pulls herself upright then, like her knees might be about to freeze up and walks over to the blackboard. "I'm not talking to you as a counselor," she says. "Really, I'm not."

I look up. She holds three new erasers from the chalk tray, stacked one on top another. For a minute she just stands there, shifting her weight ever so slightly from one foot to the other, like she is about to do an acrobatic trick. Then she tosses those erasers—one, two, three—into the air where they float around each other, moving like a fairy waterwheel in space. "Now this is art, my young friend," she says, looking with amused concentration at a far point in space, "and this is how you do it."

THE LUNA

Mrs. Woods is going through The Change. This is how Becky's mother and my mother say it: The Change. One way you can tell is that there is no water in her swimming pool, just leaves and lost tennis balls. Also she never comes out anymore, only looks at you between the slats of her venetian blinds. Mr. Woods, they say, is very good to her, comes home from work every evening. Makes his own dinner.

This is extreme. Nobody's father that we know of makes his own dinner. Not even Becky's father, when Catherine has to be away. She boils him hot dogs and leaves them floating all bloated up in hot water. Men must have hot meals, I guess. Mr. Woods gets no hot meals because of The Change.

We always run past Mrs. Wood's house because there is no knowing what she may do. Since her house is on the lower rim of the horseshoe and is down the hill we can get a lot of steam up, whether we are riding our bikes, roller skating, or just running, like now. We are on our way—Becky, Little Billy, and I—to visit Roy Graham and ask if he will take us for a ride, since it's Sunday, in his ambulance.

In his driveway is the long, shiny black Cadillac. We walk around it admiring, then ring the doorbell. Tones bounce from wall to wall inside, and off the flagstone floor and under the cracks around the door and out to where we stand waiting. Roy Graham lives alone since his wife died. Underneath his house is an apartment where his relief driver Jerry lives with his wife. Though their business is emergencies, these people live slowly and deliberately. Jerry's wife sometimes gives us cookies, does her nails, watches us eat, a smile curling up the corners of her lipstick lips. Named for a flower: Violet.

Roy Graham opens the door now, welcomes us as if we are grown-ups he likes. We bounce onto the couch. He mixes up a pitcher of Cool-Aid. It's dark inside. The blinds are drawn against the heat. Roy Graham moves around in his socks.

When we are settled with our Cool-Aid and a little plate of Oreos, Becky says happily, through purple stained lips, "Mrs. Woods is crazy."

Roy Graham looks surprised.

"Well I saw her. She stares at us through those venetian blinds."

"Lonely, more than likely," he says. He starts packing tobacco into his pipe, tamping it down with the square end of his finger.

"Her swimming pool has dirt in it too. Nothing but dirt."

"Crazy is as crazy does," says Roy Graham.

Becky has been prying apart an Oreo but stops to stare at him. "What's that mean?"

"Well, take us for example."

We wait.

Roy Graham crosses his stocking feet on the coffee table and holds the flaring Diamond match over the bowl of his pipe, sucking thoughtfully. "That's what I mean. Take us."

It seems like he is not going to say anything more. It seems like he has all the time in the world. Very gently he is crossing and uncrossing his feet, his socks making a whispering sound. Finally he leans forward and says, "Let's all go for a ride." Then he says, "See if Violet and Jerry want to come too." He is already sliding his square black hospital shoes toward his feet with two fingers.

Becky and Little Billy and I thunder down the wooden staircase outside the house. Violet comes to the door with a fork in her hand from making tuna in the tiny kitchen. Jerry is lying on the couch with his shoes off, reading *Popular Mechanics*. I like to catch a look at his feet because they are so flat they kept him out of the war.

My father was too old to go even though he went to Naval Intelligence and volunteered. Then also the army told my Uncle

David he could not join because of the fingers he blew off with a dynamite cap when he was a kid, but he drove the recruiting officer simply to distraction, my mother says, until they took him anyway. My mother knew, though, that since he blew off those fingers he had Not Been Right, meaning it was more than just fingers. When my mother says someone is Not Right that is similar to my Aunt Thelma saying they have The *Luna,* only worse.

Violet does not mind covering up the tuna with waxed paper and putting it in the ice box for later. Jerry slips his loafers on and then pretends to pull dimes out of Little Billy's ears until Violet gets fresh lipstick on. Then we all thunder back up the staircase.

In the driveway Roy Graham assigns seats. Grown-ups in the front seat, kids sitting around the hospital stretcher in back. While I wait to climb in, I look up and see sunlight glint off Mrs. Woods's front window, like an eye opening.

The back of the car smells like hospital sheets and medicine. In the rear window a red cross is painted, just above where it says Graham Ambulance Service. The powerful engine springs to life. My heart races. Across the back of the front seat the three grown-ups have entwined their arms until you can't tell whose arms are whose. We ease out of the driveway, engine throbbing.

"Now," says Roy Graham, "if we get stopped, you kids lie down on that bed and pretend you're sick."

We promise. The engine leaps, and as we speed out of the neighborhood we hear the siren begin somewhere deep inside each of us and then rise, full-throated, screaming like crazy.

This photo is large, tinted brightly by an artist. My lips are the same color as the appliqué roses on the arms of my cowgirl shirt. The collie is a rich mahogany, except for his snowy chest. My sister and I sit on our heels, our arms encircling him, pretending we're heroines in a book by Albert Payson Terhune. Behind our heads the sky over this ranch in the Ojai Valley is blaring blue with puffs of white clouds that match the collie's chest. We are breathing in the country air. Behind us, neat

PHOTOGRAPH 5

white fences section off brilliant pasture land. My eyes are alight because the owners of the champion collie, old friends of our parents, are going to give us a collie puppy to take home. My sister's eyes are dark and deep. She knows already that Mother will change her mind when she hears the puppy's complicated diet, his need for shots, and most of all his need for worming.

My sister's eyes are dark with knowledge.

Instead of having a puppy we will be driven to horseback riding lessons every Saturday at the Sleepy Hollow Riding Academy. My father is a great believer in lessons. In fact, it would be a good idea if we all took riding lessons.

Some consolation prize, my sister says.

My father buys boots and jodhpurs for himself and my mother. They go out on the trail with a private instructor, while my sister and I circle the ring with other kids. Afterward we sit high in the bleachers waiting for them to return. The sun through the jacaranda tree dapples our arms and we smell like horses and leather. At last we can see them in the distance: three dots. I smell my hands, remember the creak of saddle leather, jump from plank to plank, a pony leaping.

At last I look up to see my mother moving toward us slowly

with a man on either side. Then they stop below us and we listen, as if we are invisible.

The instructor shows my mother the correct way to dismount. She tells him she can't. My father dismounts in the correct way. She tells them she can't.

Of course you can.

She places her left hand on the pommel and her right hand on the extreme ridge of the saddle. Then she swings her right leg over the horse's rump so she is bearing her weight on these two hands, like an acrobat poised on the rings. Then she kicks free her left foot from the stirrup—in the correct way—and slides slowly down, crumpling down, all the way down until she is sitting in the dust.

The two men stand there, not believing.

Later, in the car, she tells my father she will take no more riding lessons. I lean back into the seat where my father cannot see me in the rearview mirror. My sister is staring out the window. If she looks at me we will understand too much. It is best to be quiet and just keep our own counsel. I am thinking, though, thinking about my Texas grandmother on her pony and my Uncle Lee playing polo and my grandfather making saddles. That's one side of the family; not hers.

Then I start thinking about the other side too, and about Pancho Villa coming to my grandmother's ranch in California and how my own mother was scooped up onto a horse and held by a famous bandit and then set down again safe and free, like any dog or kid.

When I look up from this dreaming I see in the mirror my father's brown eyes. Then my mother cracks her window and tells us—with a low laugh—that we all smell like horses.

AMONGST WOMEN

My Aunt Ella is sitting on the porch in my grandmother's rocking chair when my sister and I walk up the steps to the house on Allesandro Street, after school. Aunt Ella's face is in flames from the September heat and from grief. Over the arms of the chair languish her own heavy arms, each looking like a hot, dimpled child. Her bosom, into which my sister and I used to sink our blissful, infant heads, heaves. She shakes her head and sends her hanky searching up under her wire rimmed glasses.

"How's Mymama?" my sister asks.

Aunt Ella's bosom rises again and when she makes a gasping sound we both grab her around her waist. It's like hugging the equator. Aunt Ella weighs three hundred pounds and Aunt Bertha weighs eighty-nine. When my mother was sixteen, Aunt Bertha chased her around the house with a butcher knife and Mother had to lock herself in the bathroom until Mymama got home from shopping.

Aunt Ella lives across the street in a little frame house the Cat Woman used to live in. My mother says you can still smell the seventy-five cats but I can't. Aunt Ella's house is always dark and driven through life by the energy she makes rocking all day on the wooden floor, whether on her porch or in her living room. Every morning my cousin Della Lee and her father John Wesley Warner help my Aunt Ella out to the rocker on the porch, and at sundown they take her to the one inside, like they are lowering and folding a flag until tomorrow, when it is to do all over again. Book Two

My aunt is probably stuck right now inside this smaller rocking chair. But we are all holding on to each other, not knowing what will happen to Mymama, when all of a sudden Aunt Ella catches a glimpse of her husband, John Wesley Warner, across the street. We feel her chins moving up on each other and then she yells out "John Wesley Warner, you horse's behind."

My Uncle Wes has not done anything in particular but his existence has always been enough provocation. He weighs eighty-nine pounds, the same as my Aunt Bertha, and has the startled look of a chicken, even when my aunt is not yelling at him, which is only when she can't see him.

"Mama's not doing good," Aunt Ella tells us, and squeezes us again. That is likely to be the only diagnosis we will ever hear because my mother's family hates doctors ever since a doctor took out all the kids' tonsils at once, thirteen pair. My mother, who has never let anything else be taken out, says they didn't even get ice cream.

So nobody in the family ever repeats what a doctor says, and whatever anybody is sick of will likely be a fit, a spell, or simply not doing good. This last is the worst. Three years ago Uncle Jake died of it, and we went to the funeral. My sister didn't care to see him but I did. He had lipstick on and seemed more lively than in real life, maybe because of Aunt Thelma reaching in and lifting up his hand to pat it and talk to him in an encouraging way.

"Not good at all," she repeats. Then her eye picks up Uncle Wes moving along behind the uncut bushes between the sidewalk and the house, but he ducks behind a tree just in time. My sister and I go inside, leaving Aunt Ella wedged.

We sit down on the couch, wondering if playing Chinese Checkers would be disrespectful. A curtain separates my grandparents' bedroom from the living room. The curtain hangs from giant wooden rings that clack whenever the curtain is shifted this way or that, clack like my grandmother's bracelets when she raises and lowers her arms.

Inside is always dark and so small the foot of the bed almost touches the wall. There is a chest against the far wall and near the curtain an altar to the Virgin with a little candle. The Virgin herself is plaster of Paris, painted with red lipstick and a blue shawl. We hear our aunts inside the tiny room saying Hail Marys together but so softly you can hear their beads moving too. "Blessed art thou amongst women," they say.

We go into the kitchen. Aunt Maggie is stirring a great pot of beans. "Hello honey girls." She wipes her hands on her white apron and makes for us. She smells like face powder. Her eyes glint almost black inside the brown circles of skin, before the powder begins. She looks like an owl. Aunt Frances is sitting at the table. Aunt Frances always calls me the little teacher, but today she forgets.

My Uncle Ukie is standing at the kitchen sink drinking tequila out of a jelly glass and licking salt off his arm. "Never look back," he says. Mypapa looks at him, his lips staying in a white, thin line, almost like the scar on my sister's knee. He is German, they say, but not like the ones in the war. Different.

Light is reflecting off his glasses so they look blank. Like two big zeros. David Elmer Shrode. He sits straight and his clean hands are folded in front of him. Though I am too far from him, I know he smells of soap. He sighs but his lips don't change. Everybody is always very polite to Mypapa, as if he is not only clean but delicate.

My Aunt Bertha looks across the table at him, remembering when he was not so delicate, when his belt would come whistling out of its loops toward her like a crazy snake, but not his voice, never his voice. This quiet man. She fingers her pack of Lucky Strikes. She would never smoke in front of him, though she remembers before she left home, remembers lying in bed on the sleeping porch with her three sisters, smoking and laughing, blowing the smoke through the screen and into the night.

"Never look back," says my Uncle Ukie, sucking a lime with his crooked teeth. Nobody has made tortillas. Only Mymama does that. So my sister and I eat our beans and rice without them. Nobody else is hungry. Brother comes in and starts drinking tequila too. At the sink. They never sit down when they are doing this. Brother knows Mypapa is looking at him and gives a little cough when the tequila first hits the back of his throat.

Brother is six foot five in his stocking feet and is married to Crazy Rena, a bird of a woman who according to both my mother and my Aunt Thelma has got to be nuts to even put up with their oldest brother. Once he rolled her in a rug and left her for two days with her head sticking out one end and her feet out the other, like Rolly Polly Pudding when the rats stuffed him into the pie shell. It was in the newspaper.

Next Aunt Sonna comes in with corn wrapped up in newspaper. She puts the bundle on the kitchen table. Her two little boys circle the table. One is brown and one is light, like me. One of them is adopted but I don't know which one. They don't come over much because Aunt Sonna has to take care of Uncle O.V. Aunt Maggie gives them plates of beans and rice to stop the circling.

There is no sound going on but our spoons when my mother appears all at once in the kitchen door. She stands, holding on to the door frame. Her voice is weak like it gets when she is mad at my father and he won't discuss it.

She tells us this story: that in the candlelit room Mymama saw a beautiful lady, that she appeared in that little space at the foot of her bed, glowing like God, wearing her blue shawl. That Mymama had smiled and told them all to look, her daughters, look at the beautiful lady who had come for her at last. That they had not been able quite to see her themselves, but that she had come.

REQUIEM FOR MYMAMA:
A GREAT GRANDDAUGHTER SPEAKS OF HER ANCESTORS

My great grandmother lived in a house full with three generations of her family in a neighborhood where she was warmly respected and sought out for her friendship. As her daughters got older, her household responsibilities lessened, giving time back to her.

The one household task she kept up was the daily household food shopping. This was in the days of real ice boxes. Every morning she would get dressed up, including hat and gloves, and take off with a list my grandmother had made for her.

She would return just in time to put on an apron before my great grandfather would come home from work, keeping up the image of the dutiful housewife. What she did with these extra hours out of the house no one knows.

I like this mystery surrounding my great grandmother and what she did with her days. It allows me to invent all kinds of fantasies about her. I never met the woman who plays such a large part in my imagination. My great grandmother died when my mother was four, but she lives on inside me. —*April Fox, October 1989*

HOUSEKEEPING

I

Mypapa is lying on the bed in his darkened room. If he places his body exactly where his wife was lying when her Virgin came for her then he can almost feel the darkened energy like a flickering light bulb inside himself.

His long legs are stretched out perfectly, the creases in his work pants exactly parallel. His shoes are under the bed, of course. His rimless glasses lie folded on the small bedside stand. He does not need to see in the small room through which he can move like a blind man, his clean and squared off fingers not needing to touch the few pieces of furniture. The window is lifted two or three inches, the blind pulled even with the bottom of the window.

It is exactly seven months since the Virgin came for his wife and it is the third morning he has waked up drenched in urine. Thelma, his eldest daughter stood him in the bathroom and stripped him like a child, drew his bath, brought his clean clothes.

His hand moves across the clean, taut sheets upon which he lies in his pressed work pants, in his socks. He feels like folded laundry. Waiting.

From the kitchen come the sounds of distant conversation (the soap opera, he supposes; probably Helen Trent) and of his daughter Thelma mopping the bathroom floor. Otherwise silence. His son-in-law is at the bakery working, his granddaughter is across the street with her aunt. They are alone in the house, he and Thelma.

He reaches for his glasses, unfolds them, and puts them on, as if to read. But he does not read. He lies on the bed in the small room where his wife has died and tries to feel the energy that each day

My Mama's Mexi-Briefcase. Exterior.

comes a little more dimly through the coils of the mattress on her side. In a moment he will get up.

In a moment he will get up and ease open the top drawer of the tall narrow chest he has always shared with his wife. His clean fingers will move like those of a blind man skirting furniture until they close on something hard, something wrapped in a soft cloth (his eldest son's old flannel shirt; the green silk scarf that belonged to his mother; his wife's black mantilla) and he will set the bundle down (on the bed; on the small table; on the stool) and slowly unwrap it until the gun (the Colt given him by Pancho Villa; the German Luger his son David brought back from the war; the 38 he bought last week in a pawn shop on Riverside Drive) lies in the single bar of light from the window. In a moment, when he has enough energy, he will carry the bundle into the bathroom and close the door. It has to be the bathroom because all their shared life his wife kept only a curtain between herself and her children. Because the kitchen stands open too, and the small living room. Only the bathroom has a door.

II

Thelma is whistling as she mops the bathroom floor. Her papa is clean and resting. She glides the string mop from side to side in rhythmic looping, remembering when they did not have a bathroom, when she and her sister Juanita would run outside in the dark with their papa's flashlight, flicking the beam up into the trees and laughing with terror, playing the narrow light against the distant side of the outhouse. Shhhhh, Juanita would say, you'll wake them up. The brothers. They would come running in their underwear, scratch on the door, howl like wolves. Wild things. Boys.

She had ironed more shirts in her lifetime . . . (she stops to polish the mirror with her sleeve): there. Finished.

Leaning on the mop, she surveys. A thousand tiny octagons of white tile wink back. One day she will have her own bathroom in her own house ("Can a little girl from a mining town in the west find happiness . . . ?"). She will have pink roses on the shower curtain and on the towels also. She will have matching pink on the toilet lid and a deep soft rug so that your feet are not cold in the morning. Pink kleenex in a jeweled box.

Her mother would say froufrou. Thelma wrings the mop over the bucket, tears flooding her eyes. Seven months. She picks up the mop, the bucket, the Okite; leaves the door open in case Papa has been waiting.

PERFECT UNDERSTANDING

"Let's go," says my father, tossing me my baseball cap. It is not unusual for my father to invite me. There are places we go together, and we go there alone. Mostly hardware stores. I like nails, screws, hoes, hedge clippers, mailboxes, hammers, wheelbarrows. The smell of hardware.

Other times we go to the Atwater Public Library and each check out fourteen books. We carry them stacked high to the car, take them home, and read for two weeks, then we go back for fourteen more.

Sometimes we drive down to Long Beach to look at sailboats tied to docks or racing across the bay. One day we will have our own boat and sail around the world with me as boatswain, hanging from the mast, piping my silver whistle.

Today I settle my cap on my head, jump in the old green Cadillac next to my father. As he turns the key in the ignition I notice it. That strange humming coming not from the car but from him. High tension again.

He backs out of the driveway, his tan arm cocked over the back seat. "Where are we going?" I ask.

"Secret," he says. Then he makes that little gulping sound, between a giggle and a sob.

When we turn onto Riverside Drive he finally says, "This should make your mother's life a lot easier."

My father often has ideas about what would make my mother's life a lot easier, things she would never think of by herself, and teaching her to drive is never one of them.

He pulls into the parking lot of his barber shop. But since my mother does not cut my father's hair anyway, how will it make her life easier if he gets a hair cut?

Roberto, the owner and my father's personal barber, greets him in Spanish and me in English. Then they talk back and forth, very fast, ending in a sequence of *sí, sí, sí,* having reached a perfect understanding. I start to move over to the row of chairs for spectators, where I like to thumb through old *Reader's Digests* and *Look* magazines.

But they are staring at me. Next thing I know Roberto has lifted my baseball cap off my head, hung it on the hat rack, and guided me to his own chair. He lifts me up, snaps a clean sheet around my neck, and begins snipping. Fast. As fast as he talks. Spanish. To my father.

His silver scissors fly about me. They glint from speed and the overhead lights. Tufts of blond hair fall onto the sheet. I look at the girl in the mirror.

Roberto rotates the chair until I can't see. My father laughs. The barber at the far end of the shop looks up from his work, pauses, scissors in his hand. Then an electric razor purrs up my neck, powder flies, a soft brush whisks my neck. I look at the boy in the mirror.

Roberto reaches my cap down from the hat rack and settles it on my head. "Fits better now," he says, helping me down. My father hands him money, rolled up.

On the way home we don't say anything. The humming inside him has turned into something else. Something slower, humping like silent waves of current inside walls. I turn my head once to look out the window. No hair sliding across my collar. Instead prickling and resistance. I hold my head straight after that.

In the driveway I get out. My mother is standing in the kitchen door. When I move past her on my way to my room she lets out a little sound like a moan, but softer. As I start up the stairs I hear my father begin to explain. I hear the word "easier" and close the door.

I am standing at the waterwheel watching the water splash from the spout above onto the creaking wooden wheel, which turns in gentle response; I have been reading lately a Classic Comic Book called *The Mill on the Floss*, about a place that must have looked a lot like this very restaurant, the Thistle Inn. My mother calls the Thistle Inn a neighborhood restaurant but you can tell she knows it's fancy just by the way she always opens her thick, ironed

D I N N E R   1 9 4 9

napkin and drags it with such luxury onto her lap.

My father holds the door and we all go in. Everything is deep mahogany and plush velvet reds and candles in the dark. You can hardly read your menu. While we are deciding, Becky's cousin Freddy, dressed in black slacks and a starched red jacket, comes over and fills our thick goblets with ice water. Freddy works here on weekends and for that Mother thinks he has a little initiative. Becky says Freddy and my sister will marry when they grow up and the families will be united but my sister says impossible. He smiles and shows his chipped front tooth. My sister looks down at her menu.

Everything is steaks. Thistle Inn is famous for them because the owner is Adolph, the man who invented that meat tenderizer. He will probably come over and smile at my mother in a minute. She likes to be known, she says, it just makes life a little pleasanter.

While we are waiting for our salads my father says he has some good news and that partly we are here as a little celebration. I thought we were here because last time we went out to eat Daddy wanted to go to the Mexican restaurant where the wall is falling in and the food is so good. They put us exactly next to the worst part and my mother said this is too much atmosphere and the waitress called her "Miss Hollywood" under her breath and then the Silent Treatment began and it lasted three days.

We look at my father, waiting. His face turns red and he coughs a little, sips from his goblet. "I bought a boat today," he says, just like that. My mother is staring at him. "A boat," he repeats, as if we do not understand a joke he has been telling. "A sail boat."

Just then Adolph comes up in his white dinner jacket and my father leaps to his feet like he is very glad to see him and starts pumping his hand up and down. Adolph kind of eases him back into his chair and my father tells Adolph about the boat and about how we are here to celebrate. My father and Adolph used to play in dance bands together. Adolph lifts his finger and next thing you know, champagne. In a bucket. And Adolph is sitting down with us and the three grown-ups are lifting their glasses and my sister and I have Shirley Temples and can toast right along with them. Freddy is watching from the serving station like he is wondering what all this excitement can be. Freddy is from Castaic Junction and thinks we lead exciting lives.

By the time Adolph gets up to leave, the color has almost returned to my mother's cheeks and here come the steaks, all charcoal broiled and more tender than you could believe. My mother starts to talk about how much initiative Adolph has to invent this tenderizer and sell it and really make something of himself so life would be nice for his wife and his kids. My father is cutting his meat in that slow and graceful way he has and putting reasonable sized chunks of meat into his mouth and chewing a hundred times while my mother talks about initiative and how it's a wonderful quality in a man.

By the time he finishes eating she has barely begun. Then she says what she always does, that we eat too fast. My mother likes to think there is more to life than just eating and that if you eat fast you are not much better than a brute. She lays down her knife and fork and looks around her like the people eating their dinner in an atmosphere of music and candlelight are going to agree with her assessment of our manners.

My father, who has plenty of theories about how to do everything on the face of the earth, hates it when my mother makes judgments. He clears his throat and says, "On Saturday we are all going to see the boat."

My mother picks up her knife and fork and begins eating again. Just then Aunt Julia spies us from the piano bar and makes her way to our table. This is Mymama's sister, the black sheep of the family. Her cheeks are aflame with spirits and rouge. She leans across the table, hugging and kissing us, then sits down, putting her Old Fashion glass on the table. My father starts telling her about the boat, while she rolls a cigarette. My mother can trust my Aunt Julia to think having a boat is a wonderful idea. My father and Aunt Julia laugh and tell stories and finally it comes out: The boat is not quite finished.

"Not finished?" my mother asks, lifting an elegant eyebrow. My mother, whose mink coat has disappeared forever into the hull of a sailboat, is justly concerned. The boat, it turns out, is not even in the water.

Saturday will be a work day, my father explains. My sister and I will paint the ballast with Rustoleum. He and my mother will calk the deck. It will be a family adventure, a creation and a re-creation. And then, after he learns navigation, we will sail around the world.

My mother leans back into the deep red upholstery, watching, listening, absently inhaling one of Aunt Julia's hand-rolled cigarettes, calculating, perhaps for the first time in her life, the true and exotic direction, speed, and fathom depth of initiative.

PHOTOGRAPH 6

In this photograph my sister and I stand in the foreground, she slightly behind me. We are not touching, but we are in relationship. Behind us looms the skeleton of a boat. My father's sailboat. It is all curved, stripped boards, blotting out the sky, which is reduced to a thin band above. The hull is propped up by stout boards stubbed into the ground at intervals, then stubbed into the hull. The boat strains against the boards as if it will bow them, snap them, succeed in exploding and scattering itself into bits. But it does not.

We two are counterpoised to the boat. Reduced, but somehow not into insignificance. The eye is claimed by the two small faces struggling against the bulk of their father's boat. The struggle magnifies the significance of these faces, one brown, one white.

A closer look at the faces shows in the brown one a certain resistance to this project behind her, a project invented and perhaps perpetrated by the father. He would have a boat. They would sell their house, say good-bye to everybody, sail around the world. The world.

This girl has chosen her mother, who was content—it would seem—in her house on the hill, who loved her *olivares*, her eucalyptus trees with hands uplifted to the night sky, who adored her own mother, Della Ortiz y Cabares, who warmed herself by her, who counted herself first a Californian, a Californian first, and not a rootless thing to be tossed and outwitted by dreams.

This other girl, the white one, is wearing a white sailor hat set at an angle. She smiles at an angle. Sets her course at an angle, aligning with the dreamer self, making him more plausible, less culpable, less oblivious of everybody's needs and rights the evening he took them all to the Thistle Inn to say he'd bought a boat. A boat?

They had not understood at first that he meant he had bought a stripped-down hull of a boat which for more than two years would rest against feeble boards, straining to fall down; that they would drive to Terminal Island every weekend for more than two years; that they would sand, calk, scrape, chip, strip, saw, sew, paint, rig, and raise up that boat with their bare hands; that only then could he hire cranes to swing it over and lower it into the waiting Pacific.

But before that could happen the two girls in the photograph had to align and realign allegiances, alliances, compacts, and lazy love, a thousand times. Yet always they remain as this photograph shows: in relationship.

ANTS

I stick my thumbnail deep into the balsa wood and inhale airplane glue. It is Saturday. My sister and I sit under the covered part of the patio, next to the kitchen door. The table is covered with newspapers and train parts. My sister is screwing an eye-hook into the caboose.

I put the lid back on the glue and look into the patio with new eyes. The jacaranda is in bloom and purple blossoms have collected in drifts. My mother is irrigating her snapdragon bed. She is wearing yellow pedal pushers, straddling the brick beds, guiding the rush of water from the green hose. Winter sunshine pools across the patio washing the Ping-Pong table in dappled light. The sound of my father's oboe joins with the sun, moving in scales.

"Is that dry?" asks my sister, indicating the ladder I have glued onto the side of the tank car.

"Almost," I say, dreamily.

Suddenly the oboe scales stop. "Shit!" says my father from within the house. My mother pauses, hose in hand. She seems to be examining the air. Her face turns in the direction of the lake we can almost see. She sets the hose down and picks up her broom.

My sister begins sanding the tank car. On the delicate balsa she uses extra fine grade sand paper, her hand moving expertly with the grain. The kitchen door suddenly springs open behind her and my father emerges in a brown flannel shirt, denim pants bagging at the elastic waistband, his horn rims sliding down his nose. He is carrying the little case he keeps his reeds in, a tiny knife, a bottle of lacquer.

The case is navy blue leather with a golden hasp. My father, born of three generations of saddlemakers, has made the case himself. The inside is lined in aquamarine velvet into which nestle my father's reeds for his oboe, saxophone, clarinet, and English horn, each in its appointed place, each a perfect sliver taken from exotic shores and pared by his own hand into shapes as delicate and translucent as finger nails, each sanded and lacquered and tied with red thread, and lacquered again.

My father pauses now behind my sister. My mother plies her broom through the fallen purple blossoms. There is the sound of straw against brick and running water.

"Always sand with the grain," says my father, looking over the tops of his glasses. My sister drops the tank car. The cat meows.

"What does that cat want now," says my mother in exasperation.

"My reed split," says my father, gesturing with the leather box. The phone rings.

"Damn," he says, dropping his case, the knife, the lacquer onto the table and disappearing back into the house.

You can still hear him. Just not the words. From his tone somebody is asking for free legal advice. He is a divorce lawyer with Bunny Cohen, who once ate glass in the courtroom to prove it would not kill you. Then he had his stomach pumped. Right after.

My sister has decided the sanding is finished. The artist in her demands paint. She unscrews the lid and we sniff up the fumes. Ummmmmm. Mother moves Daddy's reed case over to the safety of the Ping-Pong table. We take stiff little brushes from the paper bag and begin painting the train silver.

My mother returns to weeding the petunias, or what is left of them. My cousin J.D. has eaten the best again. Mother always says, "Now you girls keep J.D. out of my petunias," but we never can.

When I go in the house to get a glass of water my father is off the phone and standing outside the kitchen window with his hands on his hips. This is the posture of outrage reserved for animal misbehavior and other acts of nature. I stand at the sink sipping my water. He squats down, examining the black line of ants filing up the sides of the two garbage cans.

My mother comes up behind me, watches. "Are you girls getting hungry?"

While the eggs boil for the egg salad sandwiches I sit on the kitchen counter and watch my father dig holes. Then I peel the eggs, and mother dices the celery. My father pours concrete into the four holes and quickly sets a tin can inside each one. Then he wipes his hands on a bandanna and comes inside whistling.

"What're you making?" I say.

"You know those ants that are always in the garbage?" Then he laughs, starts doing a soft shoe on the kitchen floor. My father used to be a tap dancer in vaudeville, worked his way through law school that way, played in dance bands. He bucks and wings toward the door.

"Don't you want lunch?" says my mother.

He grabs an apple and an orange from the blue bowl, laughs, and juggles them out the door again. From the garage we hear sawing sounds.

After the train is painted and drying, and my sister has left for a birthday party, I wander into the garage. My father is pounding the last nail into what looks like a tiny raft.

"You're just in time," he says, his eyes glinting strangely. We carry the raft out to the excavation site. Pipes are protruding out of the cans set in concrete. Onto the four pipes, we carefully lower the raft. It fits exactly. My father tests it for stability, then puts the newly scoured and freshly lined garbage cans down on top the raft. Steps back, folds his arms. "Now for the grand finale," he says. "Bring the hose."

I run to the side of the house, come back dragging the hose. He unscrews the nozzle. "Now turn it on," he directs, sounding like an RAF flight commander in the last ten minutes of the film.

I turn the tap and race back to his side so I can watch the tin cans fill with water, tiny moats against the enemy. Afterward we sit on the retaining wall, watching.

Through the olive tree the California winter sky turns crimson. Silverware tinkles through the window.

My father suddenly remembers his split reed from this morning. Fixing it will not take a minute. He hurries back around to the patio. My mother has already built the fire in the grill herself, fans it with a Ping-Pong paddle, puts on the steaks. She is standing there near the kitchen door, tongs in her hand, turning ears of corn wrapped in foil, when she hears behind her the screak from the Ping-Pong table as he staggers against it, clasping his reed case with one hand and with the other his flaming, crimson heart.

TEXAS TWO-STEP

I

My father is propped up in bed at Queen of the Angels hospital reading Adelle Davis—who seems to promise immortality through healthy eating—when his doctor comes in. The doctor listens to my father's giant heart for a moment, sits down in the chair next to his bed, and lighting a cigarette with evident satisfaction, advises my father to quit smoking. My father, who has never cooperated for one minute of his life with anybody in authority, lowers his book and agrees.

"I'm serious, Jack," says the doctor.

"I quit early this morning," says my father. It is now fifteen minutes past 9:00 A.M.

"And another thing . . ."

My father lifts his eyebrows.

"You've got to cut back."

"I quit this morning," my father repeats patiently.

"I mean work. You're working two jobs, you've got two careers, music and law. That's too much for any man. And now this sailboat."

My father's hand steals up toward the breast pocket of his pajamas where his cigarettes ought to be. He will have to learn to think, somehow, without them. He will have to learn to live somehow with just one job instead of two.

He remembers himself at ten, standing on the back steps of his father's house in Beaumont, Texas, playing "The Sheik of Araby" on the alto saxophone. At twenty, old Winston says, "Jack, I done taught you all I know. Somebody else got to teach you." Next night he hops a freight west. Sleeps with bums. Listens to their stories and the syncopated rhythms of train wheels rocking him toward Los Angeles. Toward Hollywood. Jack Santray Taylor, son of John Green Taylor, grandson of James Marion Taylor, and great grandson of Green Taylor, all of Alabama, all saddlemakers, all stuffed into the worn leather bag made by his grandfather that he carries with him, that he rests his head on, that he breathes-in, just before sleep.

And then it is L.A. and oil rigs and dance bands and vaudeville. It is California and radio and that haunting Mediterranean light: morning shadows and sunsets like something dying gloriously, strangely, slowly over the sea. He learns the clarinet, the oboe—asking strangers, saying Teach me—English horn, alto sax; asking strangers to teach him to juggle, to buck and wing, to soft shoe, to shuffle off to Buffalo. Teach me, buying them beers, menudo, shining their shoes, lending them ten bucks. Teach me, learning Spanish from barbers, parking lot attendants, waiters, other musicians; lying in his narrow bed some nights, reading Nietzsche, Descartes, Ernest Hemingway, *Robinson Crusoe* over and over; books on sailing, chess, religion, law. And then it is law, must be law, and law school, playing sax at night, classes by day until now, this moment, when his life seems to be splitting in two: music or law, left or right ventricle.

Hasn't he quit smoking not two hours ago and isn't that enough for any one man to give up? He looks at the cigarette the doctor in pity holds out, shakes his head, picks up his book.

II

My mother is hurrying down the hill toward Catherine's. She is wearing her peasant blouse and yellow pedal pushers; if my father were here, and not in the hospital with his heart attack, he would say she looked just like Ava Gardner. But if he were not in the hospital she would not be hurrying down to her friend's house where in just two minutes she will say through the screen door to the astonished figure standing in the dim living room light, "Catherine, quick, teach me to drive!"

My mother, who has not learned to conjugate either form of the verb *to be* in Spanish during two years of intense lessons with my father, will learn to drive expertly in three afternoons. On the fourth day she takes and passes her California drivers' test. On the fifth day she drives us across town to the Farmers Market for lunch and shopping. On the sixth day she breezes up to the Queen of the Angels hospital to pick up my father, who is to be discharged that morning.

III

He expects Catherine. He sits waiting in the wheelchair at curbside, talking to a young man in white holding his bag. When he sees his wife driving his car toward him he reveals nothing, rises slowly, does not allow the attendant to help him in. He is wearing his robe.

His wife gives a careful, correct hand signal and pulls away from the curb and into the stream of traffic. She shifts smoothly into second, then third. The day shimmers. For a moment they drive along together in silence.

It is not quite clear which of them begins to laugh first. Next week he buys her a 1950 Chevrolet Bel Air sports coupe.

Texas Two-Step/History of a Self-made Man. Interior.

"I would never ask you," says my father, dropping a raw egg into the blender and whizzing it up, "to do anything I wouldn't do."

My sister always finds this line of reasoning unconvincing.

My father is making an Adelle Davis Pep Up drink, with minor variations of his own. Becky and I are sitting on the kitchen counter, watching. My sister exits the kitchen, a library copy of *Jo's Boys* open in her hand. It is a rainy day and we both like to read on rainy days, especially if it is Sunday, and this is.

DINNER 1951

Now my father is filling an enormous measuring cup with dark brown slime. I can tell Becky has stopped breathing through her nose. Becky can control her body in amazing ways. For example, when she wants to cry she imagines her mother being run over by a steamroller. With my ambiguous Catholic background I would never try such a thing, but Becky is Protestant.

"Black strap molasses," says my father proudly. My mother, passing through the kitchen, gives a little involuntary shudder. Noticing her presence but not the shudder, he adds, "You are what you eat."

That stops her dead. Left to her own devices she would survive happily on cigarettes and coffee. She is a good cook but like many faced with the prospect of providing more than a thousand meals a year to others, she finds their interest in food a little disappointing, perhaps even disgusting. This suggestion that her essential self may depend entirely on what she had for breakfast has momentarily captured her attention.

"I am *not* what I eat."

He smiles. It is the same smile he gets when I ask him to play checkers with me.

"Of course you are," he says, sprinkling brewers yeast on top of the black strap molasses.

"Well, I wouldn't eat that if you paid me," says Becky.

My mother lights a cigarette, feels with her fingertips the dirt around the avocado pit growing in a clay pot on the window ledge, trickles in a little water from a jelly glass.

My father hates smoke. Since he quit smoking it bothers him more than anything.

"When's dinner?" says my sister, who has wandered back in with her book. My mother doesn't like it when my sister keeps reading during a conversation with her. My mother feels my sister reads too much and also thinks too much. Nevertheless, my mother turns on the oven and sets it to 350.

"In an hour, and there are more important things to life than food," says my mother.

My father is coughing from the cigarette smoke, which always seems to drift straight for him.

"I wouldn't eat that if you paid me," says Becky again.

Nobody says anything for a minute. We listen to the gas whoosh from the oven and then the ticking sound from its heating up. Then comes my father's idea. "That's exactly what I'll do," he says. "Fifty cents for anybody that drinks a glass of this wonderful milk shake." He is talking like that barker at the flea circus. He yanks opens the refrigerator, then the freezer compartment. He sets out a quart of Van de Kamps' best ice cream on the counter next to his Pep Up.

My mother seems a little tired from having my father home so much. She runs water on the end of her cigarette and tosses it into the kitchen trash. Then she washes her hands and begins scrubbing potatoes for baking. Under her breath she is humming an old Ink Spots tune. "If I didn't care, I wouldn't feel this way," she croons.

"I'm not drinking anything that looks like that," says my sister, whose high standards for how one earns one's money she will carry into adulthood.

I am secretly saving for a horse and so I say yes, I'll drink it, after the ice cream is in. He scoops giant hunks of ice cream into the mess. They slide down the side like glaciers into the sea. Then he whirs everything on high for a minute. When he takes the lid off Becky stops breathing through her nose again. I can tell.

Maybe now she actually makes this happen; Little Billy's frail voice comes floating in the kitchen window, dimmed by Sunday rain and distance: "Rebecca Blithe, Rebecca Blithe!" She jumps down, runs out the kitchen door, shouting good-byes.

My sister is gone. My mother is cutting little holes in a roast with the tip of her knife and sticking slivers of garlic into them. My father places a fifty cent piece on the counter and fills two tall glasses with the Adelle Davis Pep Up Plus Ice Cream drink. He lifts his glass like he is Cary Grant offering a toast to a beautiful movie star. I stop off my nose like Becky did and drink it all straight down, every bit. My mother has paused with her paring knife in her hand and looks at me, then at my father, who is drinking his Pep Up like it is purely delicious and he is very lucky to have such a drink. He licks his lips, shakes his head at the wonder of it.

She rubs the roast with a little red wine and crushes some herbs over the top, then punches the meat thermometer in deep. As she opens the oven door, the first yeast belch explodes out of me. She looks at my father, who is making little penciled notes in the margin of Adelle Davis. She sets the kitchen timer.

I belch again, slide the cool coin off the counter and drop it into my pocket.

"You Think Too Much"

ESTHER WILLIAMS'S SISTER

I am clinging to the mahogany swimming ladder fastened onto the side of the boat. Glassy swells roll the shining hull, dipping me and raising me into and out of the clear cold waters of Avalon Bay. I clutch the hot inner tube around my waist. The swimming lessons have not worked.

My father has always believed in lessons. Lessons for him are a bridge of hope suspended over a river of dread. You could save your life one day by taking lessons ahead. And enrich it too. You could learn to do almost anything by just wanting to and by practicing faithfully. Like him, you could learn to tap dance, juggle, play the saxophone, ride horses, speak Spanish. Even swim.

The water, my father answers me in an offhand way, is about ten fathoms deep where we are moored. He is reclining in the cockpit of his sailboat, drinking a can of beer, and trying—in a desultory way—to teach my mother how to tie a sheep shank and a standing clove hitch. My mother, who has knotted her long hair successfully and intricately every morning for more than thirty years, holds in her hand the third granny knot of the afternoon and gazes out to sea.

I do not know what a fathom is, but the giant orange Garibaldi fish look tiny from where I hang suspended. Behind me rise treacherous cliffs that crop up from concealed caves where divers have disappeared or gotten crimps in their air hoses. I wish now I had paid attention to the hairy young man hired by my father to teach me to swim last summer at Pickwick Park. My sister and I never progressed past the jelly fish float.

My father maintains if you can float you can swim. "You don't need that, you know," he says, nodding his chin in the direction of my inner tube. My mother, who is suspicious of theories of all kinds, looks up to verify that she has passed on this legacy of suspicion to me.

"Your sister will go with you," she says.

My sister, who has been lying on the cabintop reading *Jane Eyre,* rolls an eye in my direction. Lately she won't put on a bathing suit. Sometimes not even shorts. "I just ate," she says.

"Again?" says my mother in mock amazement. She is about to add that food is not everything, when we all become aware of a shadow falling over us, then a violent whipping of canvas. A sailboat is coming up into the wind, very close. It overshoots us, then drifts aft. A woman is at the tiller and two teenage daughters handle the sails. Suddenly the woman drops the tiller, runs forward, grabs the boat hook, and hauls the float on board by herself. Then they make all the lines fast and sit down together in the cockpit as if this is an everyday occurrence, which it must be—for them.

We never pick up a float under sail. We drop the sails outside the harbor, furl them, and motor in. My father sits at the helm, my mother—after several passes—picks up the float with the boat hook, while my sister and I mix them Cuba Libres in the galley below.

This is a different drill altogether. I hear the woman in the boat moored on the opposite side of us say to her husband, "Now don't you feel like a dumb son of a bitch?"

My mother, who is more of a diplomat, says of the newcomer, "She certainly is fat," in the same tone she uses when she is lamenting the condition of Mrs. Roosevelt's teeth while praising her wonderful intelligence.

Somehow the arrival of this boat seems to reconfigure our little area of the harbor. The man with the outspoken wife is so discomposed that when he gets ready to mount the outboard motor onto his dinghy, he misses his footing and hurls the engine overboard.

I use a face mask to help him find it, swimming in light chop, forgetting my inner tube entirely, thereby proving one of my father's theories. My sister puts on shorts and rubs her legs with Baby Oil, lies basking in plain view. When old Carl the abalone man comes with the steaks he will clean and pound for our dinner, my mother ties off his skiff with a faultless clove hitch. Later my father sautés the abalone steaks in butter, tosses a salad, heats garlic bread in the oven, cleaning up behind himself.

We sit in the cockpit, eating, listening to silverware clinking companionably in the boats around us. The sun slips toward the cliffs. On a small boat near the pleasure pier a Scot in old blue jeans paces up and down, piping the sun to rest. A few riding lights come on. We sit holding our empty plates in our laps.

It is then they all explode onto deck: the mother, the daughters, and behind them a slender, silent father. The women are wearing bathing suits. Kerosene lamps from below backlight rounded arms, magnificent thighs. They dive off the side straight into those ten fathoms of water. Phosphorus edges their curving strokes. They glow in the dark.

The next morning my friend Barbara Big Feet guides her yellow life raft around the stern to where I am scraping into the water the undercooked bell peppers my father has sliced into my scrambled eggs, and watching fish gobble them.

Barbara Big Feet, named by my mother for her enormous feet whose size is enhanced by the fact that her feet stay yellow all summer from the oozing dye of her life raft, leans toward me and says, "Did you see them?"

"See who?" says my mother, sticking her head through the hatch and staring at that part of Barbara's anatomy for which she has been named. "See who?"

"The people on *The Freya*," says Barbara, shipping her blue aluminum oars and pulling herself around to the boarding ladder.

My father always knows when Barbara Big Feet's sharp aluminum oars are about to dig into the immaculate white paint on the side of his boat, and he therefore comes flying onto deck to avert disaster.

"What's a freya?" I say.

Barbara Big Feet seats herself next to me in the cockpit and picks up my sister's abandoned plate of eggs.

"Freya was a goddess," says my father, tying off the raft and stringing thick bumpers along the side for protection. "A Norse goddess."

"*Freya*'s the name of their boat," says Barbara Big Feet, polishing off the eggs.

"Whose boat?" says my sister, who has been leaning against the main mast reading *Thirty Days to a More Powerful Vocabulary*. "Whose boat?"

"That's what I'm trying to tell you," says Barbara Big Feet, who is taller than my father when she stands up straight, as she now does, and runs a grubby hand through her stringy blond hair. "That's Esther Williams's sister and Esther Williams's two nieces. Right there. Next to you. On *The Freya*."

"What's Freya the goddess of?" says my mother, setting aside her granny knot and looking at the sleek boat next to ours. Our boat is fat. We had to have a fat one so we can sail around the world when my sister and I get old enough to crew.

My father is trying to remember what Freya is the goddess of.

"Love and Beauty," says my sister, who has been reading mythology in secret. My father looks at her in stark astonishment, the way he does whenever she knows something.

"Their boat is named for the goddess of Love and Beauty?" says my mother.

Our boat is named *The Bojac,* Bo for my mother and Jack for my father. Bo comes from: Bonita, Bo Peep, and Bony. My father wanted to name our boat *Mama's Mink* but my mother said she failed to see the humor.

"Their boat is named for Love and Beauty," repeats my mother, as if there is something my father is supposed to say back to her.

Instead he turns to my sister and says, "How did you know that?"

We all stare at my father.

Just then the woman from *The Freya* comes up on deck balancing a plate piled high with slabs of french toast. She waves at us with her free hand.

"But she's fat," says my mother under her breath to no one in particular. We all wave back.

Esther Williams's sister sits on the boom eating her breakfast and looking across the island as the morning sun just strikes the red tile roof of the Wrigley mansion. Then her daughters come up on deck with their french toast. All three are wearing dark tank suits. Their hair is short and wavy. Thick looking, from wind and salt. Their feet are bare. Everything about them is big and apparently accidental.

When they finish eating, the younger daughter calls over to us, "Want to go swimming?" She is maybe fourteen. Her whole body is covered in soft blond fuzz that catches the sun; she looks outlined in neon.

"You've just eaten," my father tells us.

"Let them go," says my mother in a voice my father does not quite recognize.

He lifts his right eyebrow.

"I said let them go."

GAMES OF CHANCE

My sister and I are walking home from school with Pig Nose. When we round the horseshoe there it is again, the sign saying: For Sale by Owner.

"You moving?" asks Pig Nose.

Our father does this all the time. Puts up the sign. Takes it down. We never know when.

"We're moving to Mexico," I tell Pig Nose. "Or maybe we're going to sail around the world."

"How come?" says Pig Nose, reasonably.

"We're not," says my sister, trying to slide the ribbon up on her pony tail before Mother sees her.

Just then Mother appears, sweeping her way through the big double doors in front we never use. She looks up and her eye falls first thing on Pig Nose.

Pig Nose is the girl who used to beat me up every day after
school until we found out we really liked each other a lot. When

she comes over I am supposed to keep her outside, which is fine because that's where we'd all rather be anyway. We play poker with Daddy's chips or Ping-Pong or read in the Electricity Tree.

"Play outside," says my mother.

"The house is for sale," declares my sister.

"Well . . ." says my mother.

Nobody comes to see the house much but when they do Mother shows it because my father says why pay a realtor all that money anyway. I remember a lady saying, "Red tile roofs are so beautiful." My mother said, "Yes until one of those tiles slides off and hits you right on the head."

Pig Nose waits outside while I change my clothes. When I come out she has taken my pet rat out of the cage and is stroking it. My father is sitting on the patio swing discussing Jesus with that same man who once a month tries to sell him a *Watchtower*. The man looks tired and keeps his eye on my rat. Finally he gets up to go and my father continues his discussion on the limits of Christianity with Pig Nose.

My father says Pig Nose is very intelligent, and my mother says she is very dirty. After listening to my father awhile Pig Nose says she has to go home, and my father and I start looking for his poker chips, which he needs for his poker party tonight but it turns out they are in my grandmother's night stand.

"I can't think how they got there, John," my grandmother says absently, staring into the drawer where she keeps her magnifying glass and old letters tied up with ribbon. My mother believes granny is not right anymore. My father says just because she joined Aimee Semple McPherson's Foursquare Gospel Church does not mean she's crazy. I never said crazy, says my mother. She's just not right.

When Granny puts stewed prunes on plates for my sister and me at breakfast time, she'll say, "Well, let's see how many dead soldiers you can make." We eat them down to the pits and arrange them in a line on our plates: dead soldiers.

Now, she does not know how my father's poker chips got in her room. She wrings her hands. Then we hear my sister's voice calling up the stairs and through the door. "Are you there," she is asking? We're not sure who she means. My father opens the door and my sister tells him she has decided to try out for Ramona in the school play. He says, No, we'll be leaving the country soon, and rushes off with the chips to get ready for his party tonight.

The three of us stand there. "Are we going somewhere?" asks my granny.

That night Catherine makes hamburgers for all the kids and we play Parcheesi until Little Billy falls asleep on the floor. When my sister and I walk up the hill in the dark we can hear laughing coming out of our own living room: the poker party.

Mother lets us in through the kitchen door. She's cutting up tiny sandwiches and putting them in circles on a tray. "Go kiss your father goodnight," she says.

My sister is still mad about the For Sale by Owner sign and says she's too tired. I pick up the tray and carry it to the door of the living room. It feels like the door is bowing out toward me, like there is something blowing against the door from inside. I almost knock, but it seems strange to be knocking at my own door so I just open it.

Inside is so smoky I just barely see my father sitting at one of the two tables. Everybody has sweaty looking drinks next to them with little knit coasters on them, like the glasses are wearing damp clothes. There are bowls of nuts and olives. I stand holding the tray. Some of the men I know. Joe calls to me, and Hank. Then my father gets up and takes the tray. He kisses me goodnight.

I follow the stream of air out the door. As I am pulling it closed behind me, it opens back up. Hank is standing in the doorway, saying "Haven't you got a goodnight kiss for your old Uncle Hank?" He smells like cigarettes and bourbon. My heart says run.

Next thing I know I am running, not toward the house but around it, outside—I don't know why—but I do. Behind me I hear him running too. I step behind a bushy cyprus, in the dark. He stops. Walks toward where I am standing, not breathing. I can hear my heart, am afraid he can too. At my back is the horseshoe, in front of me the tree, then him, standing between me and the house. And suddenly I can see all this, like it's a Monopoly board I'm floating over, flying maybe. The horseshoe, the house, small lights and distant voices, the girl standing in the dark.

Finally I hear his steps leaving, hear the door to the poker party open and close behind him, like a breath let go. I never tell anyone.

Granny is leaning on her crutches, stirring the white rice she is cooking for my sister and me. Clouds of steam rise around her thin white hair making it look steamlike and ethereal. She is telling about her son Lee, after whom I am named, who looked so fine in his jodhpurs and sat a horse better than she herself ever did. There is a picture in our living room of my handsome uncle sitting calmly on his polo pony, holding his helmet and his mallet

PHOTOGRAPH 7

in his hand while the photograph is being taken. He looks aloof and aristocratic, though he is probably there because his father makes the best saddles in three counties and because—like my father—he is handsome as a movie star.

My mother always calls him my uncle who drank himself to death, though she says this with a certain regret, as if for lost beauty. Perhaps on the afternoon she went into labor with me she paused in the living room before the photograph, attracted by the honest, sensitive, movie star face. She may have said, O Lee, oh Sheila Lee, and so, in this momentary swoon over the forbidden and impossible, named me.

As Granny weaves her story of Lee and his equestrian gifts, I see my uncle's polo pony stumble, see him fly into the blue Texas sky, see sunlight glint off his useless but nevertheless attractive white helmet as he arcs toward the ground and certain doom.

"Watch what you're doing," says my father, rescuing the bowl of steaming rice from my hands and setting it on the dining room table. Then he sits down across the table from me and asks me how you say "rice" in Spanish. My sister sits down, sullen. He turns to her and says, "*Dígame en español.*" My grandmother comes up behind me and shakes a heaping tablespoon of sugar onto my rice, hands the sugar bowl to my sister.

My mother, passing through the dining room with a basket of

unfolded laundry says, "Padie, she doesn't need that." My grandmother withdraws her hand as if she's been scalded.

My father looks at my mother. "*Arroz,*" he says.

She lifts her beautiful arched eyebrows as if they are Spanish
accent marks, carries the basket out of the room and continues
on to their bedroom. He follows, as if she has told him to. As if
she has told him not to.

My sister and I sit eating our rice with Granny, who holds
her spoon suspended, looks toward the high tension tower and
perhaps to the lake beyond. "Well," she says, "the show's over
and the monkey's dead."

After the closing and the opening of the bedroom door that
day my father grows preoccupied. Now the two of them move
slowly through time like two fish in a large aquarium. They extend
elaborate courtesies to each other but do not speak. The only
daily sound emanates from the latest stray cat whom my sister
and I feed in secret and who hangs over the roof's edge,
meowing in windows until we all begin to dream the sound.

My sister and I spend more time outside: scaling crumbling
cliffs of sandstone, tied together with a jump rope; riding our
bicycles at breakneck speed through neighborhoods we've
never seen; climbing through skeletal new houses and jumping
out upstairs windows.

Finally my father says, "We've found a home for her."
We think he means the cat.

Next Sunday after breakfast we all get in the car, Granny
between my sister and me in the back seat. Granny's two big
suitcases are in the trunk. She puts one sun-spotted hand on my
knee, one on my sister's, as if bracing herself for great speed. We
back slowly out of the driveway. At the last bump backward, I feel
like my Uncle Lee, tossed into the sky by some drunken pony.

LA GALERÍA

Girl's Dream

Night Closet

◀ *Homage to a Tree House*

Good Dog/Bad Dog

Cowgirls Don't Wear White Gloves. Interior.

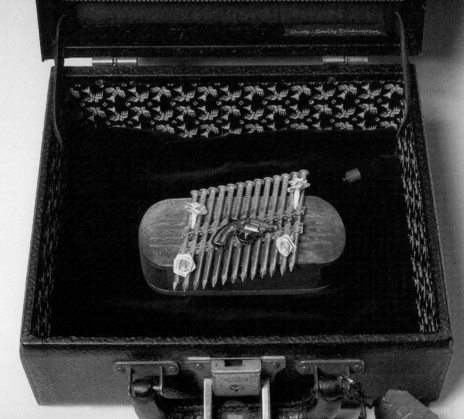

MY LIFE HAD STOOD A LOADED GUN ...

Quote: Emily Dickinson

My Mama's Mexi-Briefcase. Interior.

◀ *Winifred, Her Story. Interior.*

Recuerdos para los Abuelitos

Catch the Wave

El Músico y la Dama. Interior.

Fly Away

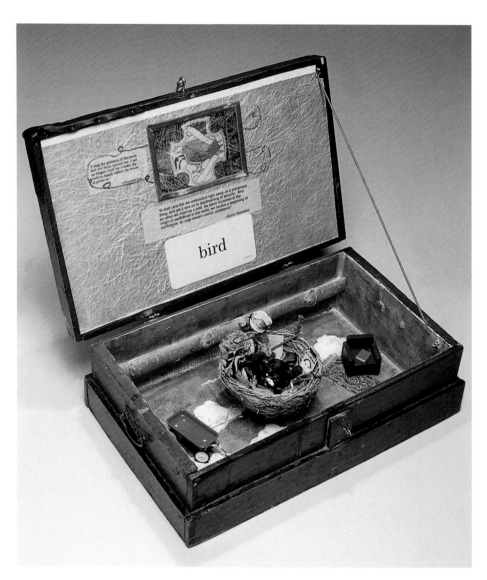

House of Pictures. Interior.

Ofrenda for a Maja

Pelorus

BOOK THREE

HEARTS

I

Under a dome of Catalina stars my father's sailboat dips softly, secured by mooring lines. Below deck my father's hands flicker over the breakfast nook table, under the *Bojac*'s kerosene lamp, until all the cards are dealt. My mother and sister are finishing up the dinner dishes, slowly. My father is impatient to begin the nightly game of hearts. He snaps on the ship-to-shore. Voices of a woman and a man talking are all but buried in oceanic static; then suddenly the universe clarifies and the woman is saying how she misses him, how her body craves his, how the clamor in her blood . . . Then she drowns in an ecstasy of buzzing.

"She didn't know," says my mother.

"Didn't know what?" snorts my father.

"How it works, that everybody and his brother could hear." She takes her place at the table, picks up her cards.

My father looks at my sister to see if she has understood. My sister flicks a membrane over her eyes, arranges her cards into suits.

In a moment my mother will say, "How do you play this game?" The question will irritate my father less than one might expect. He can afford patience because he is planning how he will, instead of avoiding all hearts, actually garner every single one, thereby not merely averting disaster from himself but bringing it down threefold on all our heads.

"How do you play this game?" asks my mother innocently.

While my father explains the object of the game and all its rules,

I plan my own strategy. I will permit my father to take Dirty Dora, the queen of spades, who counts thirteen hearts. I will permit him to take every heart, save one. Coming close but not succeeding in taking all the hearts will cost him dearly. I and only I will be able to stop him, because I have been working on my powers, learning how—by focusing with a steady intensity—to control inanimate objects, such as the dice in Monopoly.

My father takes the first trick, a heart included. "He's going for them," says my sister sullenly. He keeps the lead. My mother, who has no diamonds, keeps sloughing hearts. My mother is a purely intuitive card player. While my father keeps a running tally of which cards have been played and by whom, my mother plays each round as if it has no history and will have no future. She usually wins.

"I'm hungry," says my sister.

"You just ate," says my mother.

I am watching my father, summoning my powers, waiting for the right moment to stop him with a single heart. I fill the small cabin with my energy, but it is only a prelude to what I can do.

"What's that?" says my father, suddenly alert.

"What's what?" says my mother, discarding yet another heart onto my father's diamond lead.

"That sound." He slips up the companionway ladder and we listen to his feet clumping overhead. Perhaps I have overdone it.

"Oh, my God," he says.

We drop our cards and scamper after him. There is a purple red light in the north and a sudden, heavy chop. The wind keeps changing direction. My father, leaning over the bow talking with a man in a skiff, turns and shouts back at us, "Storm coming." He helps the man shove off, then pounds back down the hatchway and turns on the ship-to-shore. We follow, slide back around the table. There is a squealing; the airways are overloaded. Finally the nasal voice of the San Pedro marine operator breaks through in dire warnings.

I look with delight at my sister. We relish rough weather and disaster. My mother zips up her Amelia Earhart jacket and says, "We're leaving."

My father hesitates. Because he was too old to join the navy in World War II he has some vague inclination to go down with his ship now. But honor, like the game of hearts, is a concept alien to my mother. She begins to pack a duffel bag.

The boat by now is pitching and rolling. The harbormaster, moving among the moored boats in his wallowing launch, is announcing through a bullhorn that everybody should set storm anchors and go ashore.

"Where are the storm anchors?" asks my mother.

My father likes always to give the impression that he is the kind of person prepared for any eventuality. There are, for example, two first aid kits on board, as well as a war surplus inflatable raft that includes K-rations and primitive fishing gear for six people. In the glove compartment of his car, twenty-six miles away on the mainland, is a snakebite kit.

"We don't have any storm anchors," he says, and whistles into the wind for a shore boat.

But they are overworked. While we wait, he and I double the mooring lines and make everything fast on deck. My mother and sister screw tight the portholes and secure the hatches. At last a single ghostly shore boat struggles in our direction, castaways hanging from every line and life rail. Slowly we make our way toward the lights of Avalon.

II

They are lucky to get a room in Island Efficiencies. It is high season, though Island Efficiencies usually has vacancies even when elegant hillside hotels with views of the cliffs, the bell tower, the Wrigley mansion have been booked for months. But the storm has blown Island Efficiencies extra trade, people like the family sleeping in Unit 5, who are lucky to have a place at all. Lucky really to be off the beach, where thirty-foot waves now engulf the sea wall and even the promenade.

They are safe inside Unit 5, lying on sheets bleached, starched, and ironed by Celeste's Island Laundry, and stretched across and tucked in by Melissa Vargas, who used to work in a hospital on the mainland before she met Ramón near the base in Long Beach, married, and moved here after the war.

Ramón, yard man and handyman at Island Efficiencies, had wheeled in the two cots, dragging them squeaking and resisting through the rain and wind to Unit 5, where Melissa had made them up for the hollow-eyed children while their parents stood, dripping onto broken linoleum.

It is almost an hour later and everybody has had a hot bath and Melissa Vargas and Ramón are making love in their snug cottage on Clemente Street, and the family from the boat are lying in the dark under tight sheets listening to rain drum the roof, while wind embraces and releases Unit 5 in passionate huffs and impulses.

In her cot by the door the elder daughter is thinking about how she never got a chance to join the Girl Scouts because of her father, who was always about to sail around the world, who was always putting a For Sale by Owner sign in the front yard, and who never let them take a free and easy breath in their lives. If she was a Girl Scout she would survive this storm alone in a cave somewhere and in the morning, when everything had dried up and eased down, she would emerge, new and sure, and eat berries and wild mushrooms without dying, because she would know how.

Her father, on the opposite side of the room is wishing he had bought insurance for his boat and wondering if it is too late now. But if he were to get up, ever so quietly, to make a phone call or two, his wife would wonder where he was going and there was no reason now to let her know that the boat was not insured. She did not understand these things, business, and the importance of insurance and having a plan for everything. Sometimes he worried what she would do without him, although he has stopped smoking, reads Adelle Davis, and drinks Pep Up almost every day. Still a man has to think about these things, about the frail family he holds in the palm of his hand. About the dangers of ordinary living, and the extraordinary living he sometimes finds himself doing, and suddenly he sees his boat dragging free of its mooring lines, drifting directly toward the rocks and he, lying helpless under tight sheets instead of going down with his ship, as was right and honorable. He wrestles his right leg out of the sheet and just as he is about to stand, his wife's cool hand seeks him out and he sits back down on the side of the bed, defeated.

He is restless, she thinks, never able just to turn out the lights in his head and go to sleep. She could dim hers at will, like all her family, could go whole days without thinking of anything at all. Dark and still. She hears him lie down and draw his leg back under the starched sheet. (Her own family philosophy: *Never look back*.) She listens to the rain on the roof and the drumming of her husband's thoughts. (The cosmic view: *What will be will be*). Then he says one word: insurance? Ah, she sees now his vision of the boat on the rocks. But what, after all, was insurance? A piece of paper.

(In nine years she will marry a man who sells insurance for a living. He might as well be a magician).

In the next bed the younger daughter, as if she is watching a platform diver, feels her mother's stylized long drop into a pool of sleep. Forces gathering in the dark now, the girl can hear the laboring engine of her father's heart, can see with him their drifting, blind boat plunging toward rocky cliffs, while below deck unplayed cards lie scattered on the darkened table.

CALIFORNIA RANGERS

I straighten my tie and look down the dark main corridor of the Sleepy Hollow stables. Every twenty feet or so a naked bulb hangs from a cord, lighting up a bubble of air just so far and no farther. The corridor looks like some kind of long human organ, the alimentary canal or something. Which is why my sister usually doesn't come, why she spends her Thursday nights at home drawing horses with colored pencils. That's why she was not promoted. I slide my hand over the chevron on my military shirt that proclaims my rank in the California Rangers: private first class.

At the far end of the stable a horse backs out of a stall. A short girl in khaki jodhpurs and tall boots leads her horse slowly under the string of lights toward me. He is blowing his lips against the feel of the cold bit in his mouth. I start down the corridor toward them.

"P.U.," says the girl, holding her nose.

Actually my sister is right when she says I like the way it smells
in here. What I don't like is walking alone into the dark, narrow

stall and slipping past Gin Rickey's twitching ass, and his flicking tail; how he stands on one back foot and then the other barely containing his impatience, the most lively thing about him.

But I announce myself, like Major Law told me always to do, by sliding my hand along his flank as if I own him. In the dark I am moving quick and like I know what I am doing. I slip the bridle over his head and whack the bit against his closed teeth. He opens, fooled for a minute. I buckle the strap under his chin and spread the saddle blanket across his fat back. He is starting to balloon his stomach so that when I cinch the saddle on it will be loose, maybe fall off later when Colonel Maurat gives the command: canter, ho. More than once I have seen riderless horses triumphantly wearing saddles around their bellies, their backs free. I drag the saddle from the stall divider and throw it up on top the blanket. In the next stall I hear pee starting to fall from a great height.

By now Gin Rickey and I are both holding our breath. I get the cinch in place, then smack him hard and sudden in the gut, and when he breathes in, surprised, I cinch him up tight. As I lead him off to the mounting block I feel little puffs of breath on the cuff of my shirt.

This may seem like an easy win but not really. Twice Gin Rickey stepped on my foot. Once he bit me. Once he kicked me. On a single night this horse threw me six times and I was written up in the *California Rangers Bulletin* for it.

I wait at the block now while another short girl mounts. When I achieve my true height I will be able to spring up from the ground. Like Barbara Benson.

Barbara Benson is a captain in the Western Division. I am in the English Division. Like everybody in Western, she wears Levis, cowboy boots, a blue military shirt open at the throat, and a white cowboy hat; rides western. I wear jodhpurs and this shirt and tie, dumb little boots; ride English. She has her own horse, an Appaloosa. Everyplace she goes she rides fast, like there is no tomorrow.

Gin Rickey plods toward the ring, his nasty ears laid back. The stadium lights are on and moths flutter inside thick beams. Parents are in the stands. I see my mother smoking a cigarette, talking to somebody's dad. The collar of her coat is pulled up and she turns her head with an arch to her neck, like Barbara Benson's horse.

I kick Gin Rickey to see about a little speed but he turns and looks at me as if I have lost my mind. Rented horses. I am saving for my own, though, packing turkey dressing every Saturday all day at Van de Kamps bakery. Then finally my father can stop pretending every Christmas that he's bought a horse for me. "Oh Christ," he always says, "I almost forgot to feed the hor—"

Under patterns of dark and light we begin forming our two divisions. I rein and kick my way into place inside my platoon. Barbara Benson is on her Appaloosa in front of the Western Division. Her leg is flung carelessly around the horn of her saddle as she sits at her ease talking to her first lieutenant, and I know before I even look at Colonel Maurat that he is regarding her with disgust.

Colonel Maurat has a glass eye and medals all over his chest. The thing he cannot stand is if people ride like cowboys. Really he prefers the English Division, whose uniform he himself wears. In the English Division we sit tall and ride with heels down and toes out, our elbows close at our sides at all times, reins held close to the saddle but never touching it.

Always after we ride, we all go to the dark little log cabin café where Colonel Maurat explains what we did wrong that night. Mostly it's the Western Division and mostly it's their elbows and that they gallop everywhere, shouting. He bangs on the table with his fist. They say one night before I joined he banged so hard on the table that his glass eye fell right out and rolled across the table, making a sound like a marble.

He is sitting on his nervous horse now with the white foam already beginning to coat its lips, eyeing Barbara Benson. But she keeps talking, and even flips her cowgirl hat off her head so it hangs down her back. She's beautiful. Then she is off galloping around the ring and rearing her horse up and letting her elbows go just any old way.

Colonel Maurat blows his whistle and it is clear he will have plenty to say about the Western Division after our ride tonight. He waves his arm around and both divisions start forward, first the Western and then the English. Colonel Maurat will ride with the Western division and Major Law will ride with us. Major Law is tall and distinguished and looks like he played in war movies. It is Major Law who helped me up all six times Gin Rickey threw me that night, and who folded his hands into a stirrup and hoisted me up onto his back over and over. That last time we were both so tired he threw me clear over the horse and into the dirt.

We ride past the parents, holding our elbows close in and the reins low in our left hands. My mother gets up and gestures to say she will meet me afterward in the café. She hugs herself to show she is cold, needs coffee.

We follow the broad trail toward Los Feliz Boulevard. Traffic is always fast, even at night. Major Law and Barbara Benson stop the cars. Each of them sits between us and one direction of the traffic, a defending arm upraised while we clop, clop slowly across the asphalt, two abreast. The people in their cars look surprised to see horses in the city at night.

On the other side of the street we move off pavement into soft dirt: the bridle trails. They wind all through Griffith Park in ways that only our officers understand. The command comes to trot. I kick Gin Rickey but he won't move until all the horses around him are trotting. He's thinking probably about the way home and how once his head is turned the right way that then I'll see some fancy foot work but not until. Once he tried to scrape me off on a tree. Fat chance.

Major Law says to canter. That's like shifting gears: you kick and give a quick pull on the reins and suddenly you are rocking along, easy but fast. Even Gin Rickey likes a good canter, if it's not too long.

It's a funny night. We're deep in the park now. No headlights. No lights at all. No moon. No stars. Nothing to see, and the only sound on the thick air is the whuf, whuf of horse parts and people parts, tack, and saddles, all moving along in this rocking way.

Then the command to walk. Just in time. Gin Rickey was starting to gear down into a trot every now and then to say that's enough. Now he walks along, blowing his lips and pretending to stumble. I yank up on the reins because if you give in even a little with this horse, next thing you know he decides he's itchy and will roll on the ground.

The major says to halt. I hear a horse behind me start to pee. I turn in my saddle but can't see a thing. The thickness in the air has turned to fog. Peeing keeps on for a long time. I know steam must be rising, but I can't see it. No one even laughs. There's just creaking from saddles.

That makes me think of my grandfather, Green Taylor, and his saddle shop with the telescope on the roof in Texas and about Granny in the nursing home in Sunland and about how she used

to ride sidesaddle, and my Uncle Lee, for whom I am named, playing polo until he drank himself to death, and suddenly it hits me:
my equestrian history. I sit a little straighter like Colonel Maurat
is always telling us, so lost in these thoughts of ancestors and horses
I am maybe the last to know something is going on.

People are galloping all around me, as if they are after all in the
Western division and not the English. But in the dark and the fog
it is hard to tell English from Western, Western from English, like
it is all the same thing. We are to stay put, the word comes down.
Either we are lost or the Western Division is.

Somewhere in the heart of the dark park, two riders are galloping toward one another from opposite directions, impossible
to say the position of their hands, their heels, their toes, their elbows. Perhaps one rider leans forward, drops the reins, loops her
right hand in the flying mane, flattens herself level as the wind
just before the two horses collide with the impact of speeding cars.

Back on the trail where we wait, a report comes to us from
Colonel Maurat's military revolver, then another.

LOVE SOMETHING

I

"Thirty love," says my father with evident satisfaction. Then he
tosses the tennis ball high over his head and smashes it toward me.
There is a wooden sound as the ball barrongs off the wrong part
of my racket and goes flying high over the cyclone fencing behind my father's head.

For a moment or two there is only silence, except for an occasional car passing down Riverside Drive. Then my father says to my sister, who is dreaming on the bench next to the court, "Well, Hanny?" This means she is to shag the ball and that it is a world of pities she was born so bone lazy she does not just leap up and go sprinting after every stray ball.

But my sister is a junior in high school and wears a bra and just a touch of Revlon lipstick and has better things to do than play tennis with her own father on Sunday mornings. And besides she hates to be called Hanny.

My father and I wait while my sister walks with deliberation off the court and away across the grass. My father mimes his serve in a fierce arc. I pretend my racket is a guitar and strum the frayed cat gut lightly. We are in Griffith Park, the court at exact midpoint among the following coordinates: the Griffith Park observatory, where we study the movement of the stars and planets; the Sleepy Hollow Riding Stables, where those of us who still ride horses ride them; the public pool where every summer my sister and I take lessons in lifesaving, water ballet, diving; and the dry bed of the Los Angeles River where we sometimes ride our bikes, the four of us, my mother and father on elegant, slim Raleighs, and my sister and I trailing behind on old Monarchs with fat tires.

My sister heaves the tennis ball over the fence at my father. Now he has three balls in his hand, the number he likes to have. My sister and I, who have Mymama's hands, can hold only two at a time.

"Forty love," he says, then tosses the ball high again. This time I get my racket on it and give a good solid return.

Understand, a good solid return in this strange game I play with my father means I place the ball right at his feet so he will not have to run or even reach with much rigor. The object of this game is to not kill my father.

II

Observe. We have here a fifty-two-year-old man of medium stature, a little pudgy perhaps about the midsection, a man who has taken to wearing pants with elasticized waist bands. Yet for his age he looks remarkably hale. His skin color is good, tanned from sailing and playing an occasional game of tennis with his daughters.

His garage, not seven miles away, is replete with the implements of his healthful living: golf clubs, fishing tackle (including hip boots, creel, an assortment of hand-tied flies), English riding boots, bowling ball. His kitchen is a storehouse of equipment for his devotions to Adelle Davis, whose plan for eating right to stay fit he follows with zeal.

A closer inspection, however, reveals the golf clubs, the fishing tackle, the riding boots, and the bowling ball—though of their kind the finest money can buy—to be covered in dust and cobwebs, shows them gradually becoming part of the confused history of this family's life. The boots are pinned in by the grandmother's old wireless. The creel is home to a nest of finches who never hatched out. The bag of golf clubs has been reduced by his putter and seven iron, both concealed under a sheaf of comic books in his daughters' playhouse known as the Electricity Tree.

As for Adelle Davis, she knows her nutrition and has an engaging anecdotal style, but it is 1953. Adelle Davis urges her followers to eat eggs and red meat. This particular acolyte believes he has not breakfasted unless he has had two eggs, two pieces of bacon, two pieces of toast with butter. This particular acolyte believes both Adelle Davis and himself to be immortal.

If we could somehow illuminate the interior of this man's body, if the still-limited technology would permit, we would see every artery and vein coated lightly, closed off ever so slightly by a delicate blend resembling thirty-weight Penzoil.

No wonder the younger daughter will always play a curious version of tennis where the goal seems to be not to exert one's opponent. No wonder the older daughter, who always played her father with a certain tender ferocity, cannot to this day quite remember where her tennis racket is.

CLOCK TOWN

My sister and I are watching a high school girl at Foster's Old Fashioned Freeze shape my father's cone. One, two, three gleaming bulges of the white, soft ice cream. This is an edifice. We balance our own smaller versions: two bulges. My mother, sitting on a bench under a sign that reads "Smith's Clock Town," is quietly licking the single bulge that represents moderation in eating.

Nobody has ever seen ice cream like this before. Almost every evening now, after dinner, my father says let's all go to Foster's Freeze. Sometimes we have sundaes. Hot fudge cascading over the lips of ice cream makes everything slide into paradox: fire and ice. Then a cherry on top, the color of Revlon's Fire And Ice lipstick.

I lick my lips, watch the high school girl stick my father's glistening ice cream upside down into a deep stainless steel bowl of smoldering chocolate. Instant freeze. A slender, brittle brown glove. He pays. Bites in before we get to the bench where my mother sits contemplating excess in those she loves. He sits down next to her under the Smith's Clock Town sign.

Clock Town is just a vacant lot on Glendale Boulevard that our neighbor Mr. Smith owns. There are three benches, a giant clock on a post, and a phone booth. That's all. A few bushes.

My sister and I discuss Mr. Smith's madness when there are no adults present. His yard has run entirely to weeds a sure sign and a thick cattle range fence runs across the front but especially down his western boundary to divide him off from Mr. Nimms, who is also crazy. Mr. Nimms has two snarling Boston terriers with cataracts. When the light refracts off their eyes they look as crazy as Mr. Nimms. Every afternoon he takes them for a walk around the horseshoe, holding their red leashes.

Mr. Smith has four dogs. Heinz 57 dogs, Roy Graham the ambulance driver calls them. Because they are not just one kind of dog but every kind, like the sauce. Somehow these six dogs put their owners' lives in jeopardy because fences are not something they observe. Mr. Smith will look up from his dinner, and here comes a blind Boston terrier weaving up his walk, peeing carefully on his jade plant right before his eyes. Then Mr. Smith gets his gun and threatens Mr. Nimms. Mr. Nimms calls the police. The police write everything down on a little pad and afterward we all go home.

Clock Town. My father says one day this will be very valuable property, especially since Foster's Freeze. Mr. Smith already thinks his property is very valuable. He tends the walks and prunes the hedges, serious in his care.

In a minute we will all get up and drive to the Alex Theater in Glendale to watch the new Ava Gardner movie, paid for entirely by money we collected in our Fines Jar: a nickel every time you leave the light on in a room. But for now we sit licking, on this bench in Clock Town.

Cars pass. We are not far from the public library, not far from

Mymama's house, where we seldom go anymore. Not far from Van de Kamps bakery where my Uncle Jimmy Doll and my Aunt Thelma may be working right now, baking hamburger buns and icing cakes. Not far from Washington Irving Junior High School where in three more weeks I will go, carrying my new blue notebook with ruled paper and bright subject dividers.

A DREAM

The elder daughter cannot sleep. She is lying on her back listening to her sister's white rat running in his wheel while she thinks about her Texas grandmother in the home that is not a home in Sunland. Though the rat cage is out on the patio, on a table under her bathroom window, still she can hear the spinning and sometimes the sounds of incessant shredding, as the rat takes fists of newspaper in its pink claws and rips them into smaller and smaller pieces. Her sister never hears, sleeps soundly with her face mashed into Raggedy Ann's aproned lap. Oblivious.

They are in the Maid's Room now, moved the farthest distance from their parents' room, the maid's room but really Granny's room, Granny who is even farther away, Sunland and madness. Banished.

She listens, this elder daughter, to the spinning, trying to quiet her mind, thinking now of the last visit, Sunday it was, with Granny sitting on the chenille bedspread, spreading her skeletal hands and arranging them inside the patterns, saying she had made the bedspread, smiling, nodding at the sink on the wall, saying she made that too, and the faucets, made everything.

Later she and her sister pushed their grandmother into the sunroom in the chair she could no longer push herself, the chair bearing the fragile honeycomb of her left hip. Through the sunroom windows the sisters watched old ladies wandering about the lawn as if lost. The one next to them lifted her head and said, "I wouldn't be here if I didn't have to do my ironing."

The ripping sounds have started now, out on the patio. She sees the pink claws, the twitching muzzle, the long naked tail; turning in her bed she pulls the pillow onto her head, breathes in and out. But when she dreams, instead of visiting her grandmother, freeways away, she is here on the horseshoe, pulling her Radio Flyer up the hill from Becky's.

Heavy. The weight in the wagon is almost more than she can pull, and she pulls without looking. Instead she looks down at her own shoes, the heavy saddle oxfords. She watches the black and white feet moving like a machine beneath her, straining against gravity. Finally she knows she must turn around and look in order to calculate the strength this impossible weight seems to require. In the wagon sits a skeleton in clothes, her father's clothes, his captain's hat on its skull.

She sits up suddenly in her bed. "Granny," she says, heart thundering. In the dark her sister stirs, sighs. Outside, the wheel begins.

When nobody is in the dining room it seems spacious, almost vast. Above the long table the great ceiling arches. Heavy open beams offer support. Plenty of space. Plenty of windows. A whole wall of them, with a row of bright pomegranate bushes visited by hummingbirds. Beyond, the lake. Not easily seen, but there nevertheless. A flash of silver.

One can feel, almost, the sky overhead. Limitless, apparently. Stucco walls, white, with sky

D I N N E R   1 9 5 2

blue from the waist down. Then squares of thick tile covering the floor. Beautifully irregular. Handmade. The hands that made them forgotten.

Doors: three. One leading down to the music room, one swinging—with a sigh—into the kitchen, the last leading into the inviting patio.

Not a particularly warm room, but spacious and bright. Plenty of room.

When the family enters, everything changes. These people bring with them the day's events, their memories, their stories, ideas, grievances, ideologies. Stack them against the walls. Gradually the room fills up with all that they carry. Rhythmically the diaphanous walls draw in, then expand out, like lungs laboring, or like the chambers of a heart.

The whip, the one coiled decoratively on the wall behind the father's head, begins to tremble. They cut their meat, these people. Under their moving knives the long table begins an earthquake. In time the fruit under the row of windows will surely split open, spilling silver seeds.

The mother looks at her daughters. They wear her lipstick.

Space compacts around the father. Near the toe of his right wing tip rests the buzzer that could summon help. "I know what you are doing," he tells them beneath his breath, "I know you've been talking," he says, louder, as he struggles to his feet, stumbles from the overbearing room.

Alone, they are afraid to look up. They are simply astonished. Beyond their bent heads, in the distance, waves lap the concrete shore. Time hangs like a hummingbird.

DAYS OF THE VERDUGOS

"Genoa," says my father, slipping his bifocals back up onto his nose with his left index finger.

Mr. Arcucci tenderly places the salami into reclining posture and presses it against the razor sharp blade. Slices slip out the other side, stacking neatly onto brown paper. My father meanwhile wanders through the deli, his nose and fingers alive. From the ceiling hang clusters of garlic, fetid cheeses enclosed in tight-fitting wax or cheese cloth, dusty bottles of Chianti in raffia jackets.

My father handles the bread. It is warm from Italian ovens, pulsing in white waxy bags, open so it can breathe. I pick a loaf up. My father nods approvingly. Then he moves on to olives in giant barrels, floating pickles. Mr. Arcucci scoops up a little of this, a little of that. Places the swimming objects tenderly in pint size white boxes with handles, as if they are tropical fish for our aquarium. Last of all my father opens a refrigerated case and swings two six packs of Brew 102 onto the counter.

I think of my mother and the Verdugos, who own Brew 102. My mother is the first cousin of Elena Verdugo, beer heiress, who bleaches her hair and rides Arabian horses loaded with silver every year in the Days of the Verdugos Parade and sometimes even in the Rose Parade. My mother believes by some cruel trick of genetics she is not Elena Verdugo of Glendale but is instead her poor cousin, the twelfth child of Della Ortiz of Toonerville. Otherwise my mother would ride the horse straining under its cargo of silver once a year, and with a grace not yet known to Southern California, notwithstanding her unfortunate and brief relationship with horses.

My father sets down the Brew 102 next to the wrapped salami, and Mr. Arcucci rings us up. We step outside with our packages and smell oil and soap, all mixed up: Signal Oil and Proctor and Gamble. We are in Long Beach, on our way to the boat. The hatch cover needs sanding and varnishing. We drive past oil wells, dipping their dark heads to drink. The sky is overcast. In the parking lot sea gulls scream in circles over our heads. My father picks up the white bags of food and I carry the rudder for my sailing dinghy. We walk down the gangplank toward the slips. Oil floats on the water. Dead fish. Beer cans.

Since Daddy moved the boat up from Balboa Island, my mother and sister don't come down much. I don't mind the smell, though. Oil and water mix all right. Besides, sixty cents a foot is a good price for keeping a boat the size of ours.

Old Cap is standing on the dock between our boat and his, watching us. He has a wood file in his hand and a piece of mahogany. "Remounting the binnacle," he explains. He smells like paint thinner. My father waves him over with a six pack of the Brew 102. They settle into the cockpit with their beers. I lay my rudder down on the dock, glance toward Terminal Island. Not enough wind yet.

My father looks at me. "We forgot ice," he says. "See if there's any left."

I clatter down the gangway. The cabin smells faintly of salt air and Proctor and Gamble. But everything is stowed and neat, except I have left *Around the World in the Sloop Spray* lying on my mother's bunk, my place marked with a rubber flashlight. I yank open the ice box. In the upper part a slim ice sculpture remains. "Yes," I yell.

"Put the salami in there," he says. "And the olives. Everything but the bread." He dangles the white bag in the gangway. I take it. The six packs of beer appear: four bottles missing. When Mother is here the rule is no drinking until the sun crosses the yardarm. Rules get suspended when she's not. Some of them, anyway. As I am stowing the beer and salami, my eye wanders over to the open book. Next thing I know I'm lying on the bunk reading.

It's possible to sail around the world single handed. It just takes planning. I could do it. A launch passes in the main channel, and then I feel the rise and fall of the *Bojac* against her mooring lines, hear the creaking and clanking and all the responsive moves of the entire landing of boats. At sea, alone, there would be this: sound and movement, the rise and fall of swells, the keel cutting through waves, even the minute nibbling of barnacles on the hull against the possibility of total silence and solitude.

Slam. The ice box door. Have I slept? I crane my head around. The flashlight hits the floor and rolls. My father, handing beers up through the hatch to old Cap turns suddenly, says, "Make us some lunch."

A buzzer goes off inside my head like the one my father presses under the dining room table when he wants my mother to bring something from the kitchen. This has never happened before.

It's true I cook pancakes almost every Sunday morning, sifting and mixing, measuring and timing while everybody sleeps. They all rise to towers of dollar pancakes and my amusement.

This is different. I have awakened into an atmosphere of ancient assumption, strange and familiar all at once. Not until I marry, five years and three months from this day, will I hear this code again. Meanwhile, I rise from my mother's bed. Peer into her ice box. Count his remaining beers.

He comes down the gangway while I lay bread out like cards for solitaire.

"Not for Cap, just us," he says, smiling, genial. He opens a white box, extracts a pepper. "Want one?"

I shake my head no.

It brings tears to his eyes. He opens another beer, gulps. Settles himself into the breakfast nook. I cover the salami with smooth slices of provolone, look at him with intent.

He studies his beer label—Brew 102; glances up brightly. "Know what *verdugo* means?" He gives that laugh. "*Verdugo* means 'hangman.' Don't ever tell your mother that," he says, chuckling to himself and reaching for his sandwich.

When the last beer is gone we leave. He drives too fast through the night, jarring my head against the glass where I keep trying to rest it. I think I will not live to see my mother. He slams on brakes at a yellow light, skids sideways. After that he drives slower, not saying anything. I jam my Levi jacket under my head and pretend to sleep. What comes to me is this: the figure of *El Verdugo,* mounted on his silver-draped black horse, moving steadily across the dark hills of Glendale.

HOUSE OF MIRRORS

We are having dinner when it happens. Or maybe I should say they are having dinner. Steaks cooked outside over the grill, little pats of butter melting dreamily on top, grilled corn on the cob, a shiny salad.

I am on the Swedish Milk Diet, which is little dark granules you stir into milk and drink instead of eating. I have lost four pounds and am going to lose six more, but as a matter of fact those little dark granules never do dissolve into the milk no matter how long you twirl them around with a spoon. So now I just eat them dry out of a bowl. Crunch, crunch.

It's then my father says something about my nose. I run to the bathroom right after, to look at my nose. I pick up the mirror Granny gave us with the hunting scene on it and hold it out so I can see my nose side view in the medicine cabinet mirror. First I get the magnifying side and almost scream. Then I turn it right and I see it: a hook nose. This nose looms.

It is not my mother's nose. My mother has a significant nose. It looks like a Spanish dancer's nose. My uncle Jimmy Doll has it too. They look like gypsies, which would be fine with me, but mine is not a gypsy nose but a simple hook, maybe with a Taylor spread in the nostrils. My nose is the unhappy issue of a union between two antithetical cultures.

By now I am sitting in the sink. There are no decent mirrors in our part of the house; my parents have them all. "Look at this," I demand of my sister, who is lying in the next room on her bed reading *The Stranger.*

"At what?" she asks, turning a page.

"My nose," I say.

"You have a button nose," she says.

I look again, angling Granny's mirror and squirming in the sink. Next thing you know I am hot-footing it down to my parents' bathroom to check this out in their mirror, which has three sections to it and can show you the back of your head if you want. My father once explained Einstein's theory of relativity to my sister and me using this very mirror while he trimmed the hairs out of his ears and nose with my mother's manicure scissors.

Nobody is in sight and soon I have the mirror adjusted so I can see my nose angling off in two directions, four hundred noses west and four hundred east. They all have a hook in them, confused by the Taylor blobiness. All these noses are disasters.

My father is outside mixing Halo shampoo concentrate with four parts of water and decanting it into small bottles for everyday use. He drives across town to a beauty supply outlet so he can save a dime on each bottle, he is that cheap. Or frugal, which is the word he prefers. When I tell him I need plastic surgery on my nose he takes it calmly, just keeps pouring. I wait.

When he is done and has screwed all the caps on, he pushes his heavy horn-rimmed glasses back up on his nose and says, "In a year if you still feel the same way we'll have it done."

I stare at him in astonishment, this man who would drive fifty miles to save a dime is willing to spend hundreds, maybe thousands to fix my nose, it is that bad.

At bed time I am sitting in the sink again with Granny's mirror. My sister wants to brush her teeth. I look at the east side of my nose; I look at the west. It doesn't look that bad.

"So what do you think?" I ask my sister, hopping down.

She picks up her toothbrush, and dumps some tooth powder into her palm because our father is too cheap to buy toothpaste; then she stops to look at her teeth in the mirror, twisting the rubber bands off her braces, and brushing with a steady downward stroke.

RIVER RIDE

As if by mutual consent my sister and I had put off sexual aware-
ness until the last possible minute. The bus ride to the California
Rangers' lodge in Big Bear was obviously that last possible minute.
We were still an hour this side of Big Bear and already the Western
Division had settled along the back seat in fiercely locked couples
that kept disappearing below my line of vision in the bus driver's
rearview mirror.

My sister and I still wore undershirts. We still read Albert Payson
Terhune novels compulsively: *Bruce; Lad: a Dog; Lad of Sunnybank;
The Heart of a Dog.* All of them. In our imaginations we lived not
on the horseshoe near Silver Lake but on Sunnybank Farm with
Master and Mistress. True, there was a faint erotic atmosphere on
the estate in Sunnybank. Given the fact of a dozen or so champi-
onship collies who apparently bred, at least when nobody was looking, there was nevertheless a certain comforting chasteness in the
whole arrangement. At night Master and Mistress did not grapple
each other; after all, Lassie was lying demurely at the foot of their
bed.

In this world, all danger came from outside the compound: a
rabid mongrel, a tramp, a thief. Master and Mistress did not themselves harbor in their hearts any base, indescribable emotions. They
moved calmly in a passionless world, protected by dogs.

Mother said we could not go to the mountains; my father said
we could. Then Daddy said we could not go and Mother said we
might as well.

With a lurch, the bus geared down and we began our ascent. A wall of cigarette smoke like a fog bank drifted forward from the Western Division. Major Law had fallen asleep, his long, collielike nose mashed against the window. Behind him, Barbara Benson sat alone, pensive since the death of her horse. She looked, I thought, a lot like Mistress after the death of Bruce. Beautiful and pensive. I lowered my head to my sister's shoulder and slept.

Colonel Maurat was not there to meet us. The cook came out of the lodge, rubbing his hands down a dingy apron. Colonel Maurat was sick with the flu and Major Law would be in charge. Major Law still looked sleepy. Inside we ate enormous alumninum trays of canned chicken and noodles with potato chips baked on top. There were windows everywhere and late afternoon sun was shining through the pines and striping the tables. Barbara Benson sat next to Major Law and you could tell they were planning—perhaps with a certain pleasure—how to do things without Colonel Maurat.

After we finished, Major Law tapped on his glass with a spoon. I heard him, and so did my sister, and the girl next to her, whose name was Sylvia Woo. But nobody else did. It seemed like everybody talked louder and louder. Then Barbara Benson jumped onto the table in her boots and told everybody to listen up. Free time until dinner. Dinner at eight, and afterward a dance. River Ride at 7:00 A.M. sharp next morning. Buses for home would leave right after. She jumped down and the lodge mostly cleared.

Outside smelled like pine pitch and afternoon laziness. In the bunk house we chose beds and rolled out our sleeping bags. My bunk was over my sister's, and Sylvia Woo was in the lower bunk next to us. The Western Division had mostly cleared out, after flinging their gear around and filling the air with cigarette smoke.

We were lying there in the afternoon quiet when a voice above Sylvia Woo said, "I'm probably the only virgin here."

My sister and Sylvia lay very still. Finally I said, "Let's go see the horses." When we three were out of earshot, Sylvia Woo said, "Gross."

The horses looked half-wild. Not like the Sleepy Hollow horses, with their tired ways. My sister took a small sketch pad out of her pocket and started drawing a palomino, her favorite kind. Sylvia Woo said, "Ooh, that's good." Everybody liked my sister's horses.

Just then Barbara Benson came up, walking along with somebody I'd never seen before. "This is Rory," she said. They went in the tack room and pretty soon came out with saddles. Barbara Benson put a bridle on the palomino without even having to smack his teeth, just said something so low you couldn't make out the words. As she was cinching up she turned and I thought she looked right at me. "You won't want to miss the River Ride," she said. Then they were both mounted and trotting toward a path that led into the forest.

My sister was still working on her sketch, even with the palomino gone. I felt kind of liquid inside, from the mountains and the sunshine, and the words of Barbara Benson.

"I wouldn't," said my sister. I looked at her.

"Listen," said Sylvia Woo, settling on a bench next to the corral, "just what is a virgin exactly?"

My sister kept drawing. For a minute I thought I might have to say. But I wasn't really sure. It had never come up in Albert Payson Terhune. Finally, my sister tore off the page with the picture of the palomino and handed it to Sylvia Woo. "We have to go now," she said. Then we went for a walk. Just the two of us.

We walked a long time on the pine needles, moving in the direction of Barbara Benson. Finally my sister said, "Remember the horse we saw that day?"

We talked in shorthand, like that. I knew which horse she meant. "The one we saw with the jump rope hanging down from him? But after awhile we saw it wasn't really a jump rope?"

"Yes, that's it," she said.

"That's what?" I said, after a while.

"He puts it inside another horse."

"Why?" I said.

"He puts it inside her and then she's not a virgin any more. She bleeds because her maidenhead has been broken, and then she's not a virgin anymore."

"But why would anybody . . . ?"

"I don't know," she said. "It just looks like bad design to me."

Back at the bunk house, Sylvia Woo was lying in her bed reading *Gone With the Wind*. Nobody else was there except Sylvia and the girl with virginity on her mind, in the bunk above her. "Well," said this virgin, "it's becoming painfully obvious to me that we're the only ones here from the English Division."

"They all smoke in Western," said Sylvia Woo, coughing three times.

"And that's not all they do," said the virgin, snapping her book shut.

My sister stretched out on her bunk and fished a larger notebook out of her duffel bag. With a soft pencil she began sketching a farmhouse in a clearing. I had forgotten to ask what a maidenhead was, until that moment, and now it was too late.

"Well, I don't know about the rest of you," said the virgin, "but I intend to do something about it."

"About what?" said my sister, outlining a collie in the open door-way of the farmhouse.

Then this girl's feet hit the plank floor, both at once. Next she was digging around in people's belongings, searching under their pillows.

"Betty Jean Firesmith," said Sylvia Woo. "What are you doing?"

"Never you mind," said Betty Jean. She whipped Sylvia Woo's pillow case off her pillow and began stuffing things into it. Crinkly things. Cigarette packages. Next thing I knew I was helping her, and so was Sylvia.

It was getting dark outside. Behind the bunk house we scraped out a hollow place with our hands and then with flat rocks and bits of pine bark, digging until we had a deep enough hole for all the cigarettes in the pillow case. When we emptied the wrappers into the hole they crackled like fire. Then we covered the hole with dirt and sprinkled pine needles over the top, washed our hands in cold water under the outdoor spigot. We were in our bunks pretending to read when the Western Division began straggling in to dress for the evening.

"Well goddamn," I *know* I brought three packs of Lucky Strikes with me today and they're all gone but this little bit I've got in my Levis." She looked over suspiciously at the English Division. "We better go," said my sister. "It's nearly time for dinner."

"It's time," said a tall girl with red hair and long, dangly ear-rings, "for you sidesaddle panty waists to tell us what in hell you did with our goddamn cigarettes."

"Young ladies," said the voice of Colonel Law from just out-side the door. "Dinner."

There were candles surrounded by pine cones and sprigs of pine needles on the tables. We served ourselves from bubbling trays of hard little steaks and scalloped potatoes and canned string beans. There were pale brown-and-serve rolls and Melamine bowls of iceberg lettuce and huge bottles of Wishbone dressing. Major Law sat with Barbara Benson and Rory, who was the son of the movie star who owned the lodge and let us stay here as a personal favor.

Betty Jean and Sylvia and my sister and I all sat together and tried not to look into the smoldering eyes of the smokers among us. I was sawing on my steak when Betty Jean said, "Well, I've figured it out and we've got just absolutely nothing to worry about. They've got better things to do than think about who hid their dumb old cigarettes."

The three of us looked at Betty Jean, wanting to believe. "Well, think about it," she said, like a teacher who just knows her class is smart enough to guess this one, "what's the most important thing in the world to people like that?"

I knew horses was not the right answer.

"Sex," said Betty Jean, loud enough that Major Law turned in his chair and gave her a hard look. She leaned forward. We all did. Now she was whispering: "Somebody's about to lose more than their cigarettes."

By now people were getting up in twos and threes and drifting toward the door. We ate slowly and deliberately. Eventually strains of music reached us from the campfire stage. By the time we left, only the kitchen help remained. The lodge steps were deserted. We stood there a minute, then started down toward the campfire. We heard giggling in the bushes. Shrubs swayed and shivered as if alive. Betty Jean had been right: the Western Division had better things to do than worry about catching cigarette thieves.

Next morning I woke suddenly, my heart pounding, thinking Barbara Benson had ridden sidesaddle through my dream. Did I hear her call? I slid my watch out from under my pillow. By flashlight I read 6:45. The River Ride would leave in fifteen minutes. I raced toward the corral, still buttoning my jeans. I could hear snorting, and clanking bridles, and hooves turning in the dust. There were slaps on flanks and whistles and voices that calmed and voices that riled. Barbara Benson murmured "Take the roan." Inside the tack room were three western saddles. "I need English," I said to no one in particular.

A man's voice said, "Got no English. It's all western. Makes no difference."

I carried the western saddle out by its horn. It felt strange, but maybe even easier. Like it had a handle. Something to hang onto.

It was still dark when Rory opened the corral gate and we all moved through, like a posse after somebody. This was not like riding in the park. Almost at once we were cantering. I felt my body thrown hard against the pommel of the saddle, not like the rocking ease of the English saddle. I tied to grip with my knees, move with the horse.

We rose up the trail, traveling fast across rocks, climbing. My weight shifted back, easing my crotch. I threw back my head and let my gaze travel through moon-tipped pines. This pace felt good to me. We were moving like fast water over glistening stones; not in platoons by barked commands and confirmations.

Cresting, we dropped down again, at a gallop and I slid forward suddenly and hard, then repeatedly against the pommel of the saddle, felt a burning then tearing in my tenderest self, against which there was no help, no saying no as the Western Division let drop everything that reigned in, restrained, controlled, subdued—for hours, it seemed, when at last we stopped to rest.

I slid down, hurting. People disappeared into the bushes to pee, some in twos. I moved off, limping. Finally I couldn't see anybody or hear anybody. Insects droned in a yellow bush. I unbuckled my belt. I had never peed outside. I fitted my back against a pine and eased down my jeans. In the exact center of my white underpants I saw it: blood and it was not even time. There was nothing to do now but lean back against that tree, letting it hold me up, peeing and thinking about the strange and unaccountable ways people might lose their maidenheads and stop being virgins anymore.

In this photograph there is a noticeable change of atmosphere. The simple blue of the California sky has grown murky and faintly yellowed, like the picture on our eleven-inch Hoffman Easy Vision television screen. It is 1953. I am standing on the playground of Washington Irving Junior High School next to my friend Trudy Erikson. Jacaranda trees sprout out of our heads, but our hands are at our sides, almost as if we are at attention. I am wearing the

PHOTOGRAPH 8

navy blue polished cotton jumper my mother made for me on her sewing machine. The jumper has straps that exert a faint pressure on my new breasts. Still I am standing straight, not crumpled forward over a clutched notebook, a posture that will become necessary when I move on to high school. My body forms a neat triangle, a kind of Libra balance.

Trudy is a little taller, a little heavier, though we have both filled out in recent months, as if we are rising dough. Trudy's face is perfectly round and her hair so blond and Nordic she almost seems absent of color. Our hair is neat, cut just below our ears, and curled, parted on the left side. Trudy wears a turquoise ribbon around her hair, the only touch of color in the color photo. We stand balanced, our hands at our sides, contained by the white border of the photograph.

Nothing gives us away, we think. But the secret, of course, is in our shoes. These shoes exactly meet the requirements of the girls' P.E. department. They lace up and allow room in the toe box for proper growth and development. These shoes, these earnest-looking saddle oxfords, are polished with exquisite care.

In our separate houses the night before, we took old socks and made stark the white leather with liquid polish, and with black Kiwi wax established the sharp contrast of the overlapping saddle. Then with a damp sponge we freshened the line of our red soles. On occasion we would even remove the laces and wash them out, drying them on towel bars over the weekend.

Why? We are in love with Miss Highsmith. That's why. Miss Highsmith, with her resonant voice. Miss Highsmith who so carefully never touches us that the lack forms the very outline of a caress. For it is Miss Highsmith who holds the camera. We stand balanced—Trudy and I—inside the frame of the photograph, held at a distance from Miss Highsmith by everybody's need for focus, bound to her by an intricate network of hormones and imagination.

Trudy and I have made it our life's work never to allow Miss Highsmith from our view. We ride the early bus in the dark so we can station ourselves at the Ping-Pong tables next to the concrete walkway along which Miss Highsmith will stride on her way to the gym, after she has parked her powder blue Dodge on the street, always in the same place.

As she approaches the walk we are playing Ping-Pong, absorbed, apparently. Actually we never keep score but we are astonishingly good, considering that we practice with our eyes fixed—not on the ball—but on Miss Highsmith.

She never looks up. She passes now in her tailored blue suit. She carries a briefcase, wears hose, sensible pumps. Inside her office she will remove the sensible pumps and put white athletic socks over the hose. Then she will put on blazing white oxfords. She will remove her blue suit jacket and place it on the hanger that waits behind the office door. How do I know this? Trudy and I are her fifth-period office girls.

After a decent interval we streak toward the gym and check our paddles and balls in ourselves. We handle the equipment. Miss Highsmith comes out in her white nylon blouse with a whistle around her neck. Sartorially she is an oddly alluring combination of athlete and lady. For example, the erotic conjunction of bulky sweat socks over the smoothly textured, warm brown hose. Whistle resting on nylon. The faint moustache riding her voluptuous upper lip.

Her low voice curls around our nerve endings to inquire if we read the sports page this morning. Miss Highsmith loves baseball. We love baseball. Together we all follow the fortunes of the Hollywood Stars every day in the *L.A. Times*. Miss Highsmith's whistle, as she reaches past me for the office girls' schedule, comes to rest momentarily on the counter near my hand. Sometimes it is hard to breathe in here.

Miss Boschen breezes in. She is younger than Miss Highsmith and dates men in sports cars. Mrs. Merino is older and married. Miss Highsmith has no domestic context whatsoever, simply appears out of nowhere every morning. We never try to imagine her life beyond the powder blue Dodge parked on the street behind Washington Irving Junior High.

"You've got on the right shoes," Miss Highsmith says, drawing back her whistle with an unconscious grace. "Both of you." We study our saddle shoes.

"Inspection today?" guesses Trudy. Once a month in gym class all the girls line up under the eucalyptus trees for shoe inspection. It has something to do with health but since the gym teachers also teach us about the female reproductive system there is always something strangely ambiguous about the shoe inspections.

Girls in ballerina flats get a D. Girls in dirty oxfords get B. To get an A you have to be wearing clean oxfords with clean white socks. We never know exactly when these inspections will be. News travels from girls with first-period gym. Sometimes they don't tell because why should they be punished? Some girls keep polished oxfords in their lockers for these emergencies.

Miss Highsmith regards our feet with approval. Then we race off to first period. Algebra. Algebra is taught by the man in charge of buses. He is short and ironic. He knows girls can't do math so it's necessary to give them second chances. I usually get the right answers but I do the problems the wrong way. At the end of the semester he will give me a D and then I'll go on to take geometry from him. In the meantime he says it's not necessary to reinvent mathematics every time I work a problem. Actually, it is.

Next is English. Mrs. Haas loves my play, *The Mad Scientist,* and we will put it on for the class in a week or two. Mrs. Haas does not know I write poetry in a secret notebook at home, that the pages fill up automatically as if wired in by some kind of cosmic teletype machine.

Trudy is restless in her chair two rows ahead. She glances down at Tina Rodriguez's ballerina slippers and then at me so many times I'm afraid Tina will notice. Last time Miss Highsmith gave Tina Rodriguez a D for her ballerina slippers Tina said under her breath, "Puta."

Tina Rodriguez's ballerina slippers have a crushed look to them, like black flowers tossed to a disdainful bull fighter. Inside the shoes, her feet look vulnerable, as if some harm might come to them. Tina slides her feet forward as if she can feel my eyes grading her. She has not read *My Antonia,* again.

Trudy passes a note to Sally Steigal who passes it to me. It says:

Lisette [this is my name in French class],
Let's get Miss Highsmith to take us to a ball game.
What do you say?
Trude the Prude

Trudy is always trying to make life take decisive turns. I like things to keep on the way they always have. It is enough for me to be Miss Highsmith's fifth-period office girl and to be playing Ping-Pong every morning when she walks past. If her whistle should sometimes come to rest against my hand, so much the better. I could envision a whole lifetime of this. But Trudy must have more.

At nutrition, sitting out under the trees eating our hot cinnamon rolls, Trudy says, It doesn't hurt to ask. Anybody raised in my family would never make such a statement. Trudy is going to ask at lunch, when Miss Highsmith is accustomed to giving us our daily private and free tennis lessons. Miss Highsmith has already given up getting lunch because Trudy believes it doesn't hurt to ask.

I feel an expanding and contracting in exactly the area the P.E. teachers are always showing movies about. I am probably getting my period. At least I will not have to be at tennis when Trudy tries to get Miss Highsmith to agree about taking us to the ball game. When you get your period you don't put on shorts and run around and you certainly don't go swimming because you might die.

Luckily we have gym teachers to explain all this. My own mother thought she was bleeding to death because my grand-mother never told her about periods. My mother ran home from school and got in a tub of cold water—the worst possible thing she could have done.

Third period we are conjugating the verb "to be" in French and I can tell Trudy is writing me another note. I shake my head no. She mouths, It's not what you think. Actually the note is about her horse. Trudy has her own horse. When we go to college together Trudy will study to be a vet and I will study to be a famous writer. This note is about her horse and about the stable hand where she boards him. First there is a picture of her horse rearing up, and then there is a picture of her and Duane grappling in the hay together. The perspective is not good in this one. Actually the drawing of the horse is way better and has a heart drawn around it too.

I have a boyfriend myself or at least we go to parties together. He is neat and clean and never says anything. At parties we just dance and I put my hand on the back of his neck like Ginger Rogers does on the neck of Fred Astaire. Trudy does not bring Duane to these parties because her father thinks Duane is too old and will never amount to anything and that these are the best years of Trudy's life.

By now I have cramps and have pinned a pad to my underpants with two safety pins. Trudy goes off for tennis with Miss Highsmith and I decide since P.E. is next just to go lie down in the Quiet Room.

When you get your period you are "M" and don't have to dress out; you can just sit under the trees and talk to the other girls who are also "M." If you have cramps you go to the Quiet Room where the lights are off and girls lie on cots.

I am the only one in here at lunch. The sheet feels clean and I put one of the small pillows under my head, glad to rest because the Midol that Sally Steigal gave me in French has made me feel a little dizzy. Miss Boschen sticks her head in and asks if I want some Karo syrup.

Karo syrup mixed with a little warm water is good for cramps. In the girls' P.E. store room there are cases and cases of Karo syrup. When I'm office girl I mix it up in little Dixie cups for anyone in the Quiet Room but I'd never drink it myself. I shake my head no.

She goes to lunch and I lie back, thinking about my play *The Mad Scientist* and about being a famous writer one day and about how my mother always says, Do whatever you want as long as it makes you happy. Sometimes it feels like she doesn't want anything particular for me. Miss Highsmith says she is glad Trudy and I are going to college, that hardly any girls from our school will. My mother quit high school to paint yo-yos and trim hats. And then I think it: What if Miss Highsmith was my mother?

I have never thought like this before. It's more like Trudy's way of thinking. Quickly I put my mother back in place, see the art in her yo-yos and see her beautiful self with a red hibiscus tucked behind her right ear.

Miss Highsmith is not beautiful. But she carries a brief case. I am thinking so hard about Miss Highsmith that when she comes into the darkened room carrying a Dixie cup of warm Karo for me it seems like her quiet white oxfords are carrying her soundlessly through my own dreaming. She bends her face down so close I can smell powder on her cheek. Without touching, she hands me the soft cup.

Two weeks later I am sitting on the couch in Trudy Erikson's house waiting for Miss Highsmith to pick us up for the ball game. The Hollywood Stars are playing the Los Angeles Angels in the coliseum. Trudy's face glows like a harvest moon. "I'm so happy," she says. I think she means about Miss Highsmith. I feel it too, little party poppers going off in my blood. She says, "Not about tonight." Then she looks around as if her parents will overhear, although they left for the movies twenty minutes ago. "I'm getting married," she says.

Suddenly I see the picture of Trudy's horse with the heart drawn around it. I feel the horse rearing up in my stomach.

We are thirteen years old. Years from college. Miss Highsmith will pick us up in minutes.

At the stadium Miss Highsmith buys us hot dogs, Cokes, and programs. An organ plays "Roll Out the Barrel." Miss Highsmith is wearing slacks and a blouse open at the throat. Her dark eyes glisten like anthracite. She is explaining everything: about how the Angels' number one fan, Angel Annie, will let out a scream during the seventh inning stretch, about the importance of writing on our programs everything that happens, about Sandy Koufax warming up in the bull pen, about watching for the secret signals Bobby Braegen will flash him from behind home plate.

It all washes around me and through me. I cannot eat my hot dog. I cannot look at Trudy. I cannot understand how to make the little hieroglyphics on my program that will describe and record the evening forever. The code I see, with the clarity of a Physical Education film, is the embryo curled asleep inside Trudy Erikson; the sound I hear, the rising wail of Angel Annie against the night sky.

BIG BEAR

Peggy is lying across her bed in her family's mountain cabin at Big Bear, fitting the hook of a wire coat hanger into the hole in her Levi zipper. Peggy has to resort to extreme measures to get her pants zipped up because they are very tight. She pauses in her story-telling, inhales, and with quick steady pressure draws the zipper up to her waistband and says, "There."

My mother finds Peggy's ways unaccountable, not because the mysteries of the cult of beauty elude her but because Peggy is a Mormon.

My mother, who because of her continuing grudge with the pope has withdrawn herself from all formal religion, nevertheless has a certain desultory curiosity—though hers is less evident than my father's—about the religions of the world and even a certain lore about them. Mormons, she knows, keep great stores of canned goods secreted about and under their houses.

Peggy's parents have built their house on the horseshoe, right next to ours. Very close. My father does not like how close they are, but my sister and I feel suddenly very American to have next door neighbors and to run next door to borrow things. And Peggy comes over and tells us about the boys she knows from church and about the dances and her romance with Gary. My mother always listens to these endless narratives, delivered in a breathless and-then-and-then-and-then kind of way, monologues that end inevitably with the phrase, "and then I said wow."

Peggy's face has a wide open look to it, as if she is always saying wow to life. Her Maybelline eyebrows arch up, and her Revlon mouth forms a circle of wonder. My mother likes Peggy and her makeup and the fact that Peggy is somehow dancing out past the stockpiles of canned goods that constitute Mormonism. So when Peggy invited my sister and me to come with her family to their cabin at Big Bear my mother, with a wistful look, said yes.

Peggy gets up from the bed and slides her long fingers with the red nails deep into her pockets and does a couple of quick knee bends to make the Levis shape themselves to her body. Then she crouches before the tiny mirror on the wall to fit her earrings into her pierced ears.

My sister and I watch from where we sit on the day bed pushed up against the wall. Our father said we were not to have our ears pierced or our souls baptized—despite the wishes of Mymama— until we were old enough to make a rational decision ourselves. Frankly we both wish someone else had made these decisions irrationally, in the first years of our lives, so they would not loom so large now. Like Peggy, we would be pushing studs into our ears with light hearts and exclaiming Oh Wow over the prospects of the evening.

We are going to a dance tonight, down at the lake. Last night we spent here in the cabin. Peggy's mother made hamburgers, and then we toasted smores in the fireplace, and put paper rolls of music into the player piano and sang "My Desert is Waiting," while the keys went up and down all by themselves.

Peggy kisses her lips together onto a kleenex, holds out the tube in our direction, saying Want some? We put some on too and all go in to the living room, where her mother is reading in a pool of light from the floor lamp pulled up to her easy chair. Her feet are propped up on a foot stool and her dark hair is tousled and her cheeks are pink from the fire and from the novel she has been reading. She looks up. Suddenly I see the evening she will have: the book, the pool of light, the fire, even a dog curled at her feet. I could have this too, instead of the dance. But not for twenty years.

We get in the car. Peggy will drive on her Learner's Permit. Her mother, bundled into an Indian coat, wearing moccasins with thick socks, gets in beside her. Peggy grinds the gears, kills the engine twice. We lurch down the dirt drive and stop at the dark mountain road. Peggy looks both ways. Twice. Then she pulls out into the night.

I do not know how we will get home. Already I am thinking about that, thinking about the pool of light and the book and the fire, so I am glad when Peggy's mother asks, and Peggy says Gary will drive us back after the dance.

Because of his slender and gracefully bowed legs, Gary has been named Birdlegs by Peggy's father. I do not see Birdlegs standing around on the patio by the lake, waiting for the band to start. Lots of other people though. Older people, it looks like. "Sailors," says Peggy in her Oh Wow tone.

I have only danced with three boys in my life, if you count Terry Taylor from elementary school. These do not even look like boys. They have thick hands and heavy faces. They gather around Peggy, who has slipped out of her coat and is standing very erect in her pink cardigan sweater and tight Levis. There are pink paper lanterns overhead, catching the glow from Peggy.

My sister whispers to Peggy, "Where's Birdlegs?"

Peggy accepts a flask from a sailor, tips it back, says, "Not coming."

The music starts. My sister and I look at each other. Sailors press in. Peggy disappears. We step back, lean together against a stone wall.

Two men start to talk. One is so drunk he can hardly stand. The other says to us, "He shouldn't even be drinking. Know why?"

Though we do not feel curious we ask why. The drunk one turns away, as if out of a certain delicacy.

"Kidneys," says his friend. "Kidneys are shot all to hell."

"Only got one left," says the drunk sailor, turning back to the conversation. "I'm Kenny." He holds out his hand. It is damp and too warm. Perhaps he has a fever. Through the dampness and moisture of his hand, as he holds onto mine, something reaches me, something transmitted, an ancient and ambiguous message, hauntingly ironical, something about great size requiring a smaller being for support, something about men and pallor and sickness. He takes me in his arms, as if we are going to dance.

My sister says, "She's thirteen."

Kenny steps back, glances at Peggy on the dance floor with one of his buddies. "How old's *she* then?"

"Sixteen," we say.

Kenny shakes his head. "Well then have a drink," he says genially. He pulls a pint bottle out of his back pocket.

"You shouldn't drink that," I hear myself say. My sister looks at me, her eyebrow raised.

"So how old are *you*?" says Kenny to my sister. She turns away, stares at the dark lake. He bends down to me, says "One kidney's all anybody needs anyhow." Swigs. "So who wants to live forever."

"I wish Birdlegs was here," says my sister. "I wish I had a car."

"Dance with me," says Kenny into my left ear. "One dance. Big deal."

"I wish we were back at the cabin," my sister says.

We see Peggy moving toward us, through the crowd. She has a

look we've never seen. The wow has somehow deepened into sig-
nification.

"You guys," she says to us, breathless. "Guess what."

"What?" we say. She has our elbows, pulls us a little aside, out
of earshot.

"It's Kenny," she says. "He's only got one kidney."

"One's enough," my sister says.

Peggy looks at her. Maybe it's true, after all, about the stockpiles of canned goods under their house. Peggy turns to Kenny
and next thing we know they are dancing, moving slowly, deliberately under the paper lanterns, Kenny leaning heavily for support like a great, drunken bear.

Jack Taylor, master chef, opening cans of beans. Tonight it will be
Cassoulet Castelnaudary. He runs the sponge around the metal
wheel on the can opener, cleaning off the food his wife never
notices collecting there where it can infect the food her family
eats. He sharpens the knife. This must be done slowly, carefully.
A careless stroke can blunt the knife. Ruin it.

There is a way to cut onions. He slices each end off the onion.
Juice oozes into the board and

DINNER 1954

out his eyes. He sniffs, takes off
his bifocals, wipes his eyes on the dish towel, looks out the
kitchen window. Soon the hedge will need pruning.

Replacing his glasses, he draws the knife across the onion in
evenly spaced strokes, cutting deep but not severing, until a north
to south grid is established. Then he gives the onion a quarter
turn and begins the deep but not severing strokes until the
whole onion is scored with a perfect checkerboard. Now the final
step: even slices cross-wise so that perfect cubes of onion fall in
an even pattern onto the board. Artistry.

Timing, too, is crucial. For example, now would be a good
time to make the little balls of sausage, set them browning in the
pan while he dices the steak. And the wine, where is that? He
searches through the cooler, spinning the round shelves, but his
wife has not put the wine in the logical place. He can hear her
sewing machine whirring three rooms away but he will not call
out, can find it himself.

In the refrigerator. She has put the burgundy in the
refrigerator. It stands next to the bottle of milk, rather than
lying. Rather than lying in the cooler: the logical place.

It is important to have good tools. The cork screw, for
instance, with its little legs for gripping the lip, its smoothly
functioning wheels. He turns the cork screw deep, and using

his sense of timing, gradually and consistently he draws it up, twisting gently—not too much—until it . . . crumbles.

Dry. Dry from standing upright rather than reclining. He pours the burgundy off into his two cup measuring cup, always cooks with his two-cup Pyrex measuring cup of wine, plunges his two fingers in, fishing out the bits of cork, wiping them on the dish towel thrown over his shoulder.

Good. Good nevertheless and notwithstanding. Good. He stands at the sink, looking and drinking, sees through the kitchen window his daughters on the hill opposite, walking single file through the wheat-colored weeds, away from him. Good.

He sets down the measuring cup and washes his hands carefully. Can't be too careful in the handling of meat and the washing of utensils, and cutting boards too. He washes the cutting board in soap and hot water and sets it into the dish drainer, searches through the refrigerator for the package of sausage. Here, behind the butter.

Into the blue mixing bowl he puts a handful of chopped onion. Sips wine. A little bell pepper, he thinks. But where? Ah. And an egg for cohesion. He sets the carton on the counter next to the bowl.

Eggs. There was a way to separate them that was really quite ingenious but no need for that now. The whole thing. He plops it in, on top of the sausage and onion. Chops the bell pepper. Maybe a mistake, the bell pepper. He sips thoughtfully from the measuring cup, throws in the bell pepper. Notwithstanding.

And garlic. Garlic, the powerhouse of nutrition. Gypsies eat it. Wear it around their necks. He thinks of gypsies as he drinks his wine, looking beyond the hills to his journey, his voyage. He sees the prow of his ship lashed by waves, his daughter hoisting the mizzen, a wave curling high above her unsuspecting head, himself clutching his heart, and then . . .

Mexico was far enough, he concedes, squeezing the cloves through the grid with his good kitchen tool, little yellow curls of garlic falling onto the bell pepper. Maybe he should have sauteed the garlic. Chopped it, first. Can't saute it, once its pressed. Sticks to the pan, burns, then you've got one hell of a mess.

Garlic is good for cholesterol, blood pressure, memory. Cancer, too, Adelle Davis says. He stops suddenly, en route to the refrigerator for the steak, stops, remembering Adelle Davis has cancer, after a lifetime of sensible eating. After the garlic, the brewers yeast, the black strap molasses. He imagines her cranked up in bed, surrounded by beckoning gypsies, while he stands helplessly searching in the refrigerator.

He has forgotten what he came for. Stands with the light on, the motor running. Hates waste. Hates the way this wasteful life has obliged him to fritter time away dodging death, cowering from it even. Well, no more.

He slams the door. Then remembers the meat. Opens the door.

On the counter he places the white wrapped package. Studies the brown piece of tape with its tenuous grasp on the packet. Life was like that. Came apart. Fragile. He sips his wine.

In two years he would retire. Move the family to Mexico. The journey would begin at last. He opens the meat. Probably best to marinate it. Should have done it last night. Poker night, though. Maybe enough time now, give it a little flavor. He gets out the green bowl, puts in the steak, pours a little wine in. Then a little into the measuring cup. Sips. Life was like that. You sipped it. Savored it.

Two years. He rolls a ball of sausage with his musician fingers, stands holding it. Two years. He pulls down a plate with his clean left hand and places the sausage ball dead center. In the bottom drawer of his closet, crammed into a manilla envelope, were the government bonds to do it. Years of bonds. He had planned, thank God.

God? Why had he thought that? God? There certainly was no God. No heaven, no hell. He rolled the next bit of sausage into a ball and placed it next to the first. His wife, who had renounced Catholicism . . . No, *renounced* was too strong a word. Too active. Too . . . *deliberate*. His wife did not know how he could believe there was no life after death, doubted that he *did* believe it. That there was just nothing. He lifted the measuring cup and held it up to the kitchen light, to toast the absent, ironical god.

But something in the way the afternoon sun made a tiny star of fire inside the wine, as if there might after all be life inside, held him a moment. "Pretty," he said out loud, and drank.

RE/COLLECTION

THE KITCHEN

This woman knows the rhythm of chiles. The gas flame whuffs up, and she runs the fresh chiles quickly through the blue, feeling her nose inside crackle like the chile skins; her fingers heat but do not burn. She moves back and forth from the counter to the flame, scorching the skins, crackling them black, filling the house with the sharp smell of Mexican dirt and lizards, cooking *en un acento puro,* this woman who says she cannot speak one word of Spanish, cooking only *en la lengua,* moving with a *ritmo* that is her own. Is her mother's.

She sees her mother, pale in the casket at the old plaza church, the flames from gently moving votive candles flickering on her cheeks, her brow, her lips, her eyes filling from the acrid smell of the chiles as she flames the last one and spins counterclockwise the left front knob on her Tappan range.

THE PATIO

He lifts his nose to the breeze: *chiles relleños.* Refilled, he turns to his task, turns the tiny gold screw of the clasp for his new reed case. Clockwise, turning, easing it into place. There. Inside, the dark green velvet. He runs his thumb sideways across it. He contemplates the interior of his new reed case, moving past the importance of maintenance, the need for economy if not frugality, to the interior of the box, the interiority of it, the inside of the inside of this miniature world in which, momentarily, he looses himself. He does not know how long he stands inside his own interiority. The cosmos has eased into this reed case, measuring twelve inches square: no more. A breeze lifts the long strand under which his bald spot lies.

THE MAID'S ROOM

This room has always been called the maid's room though there has never been a maid. First the room was her grandmother's. Kind Texas grandmother, gone now. First: banished. Then: dead.

The elder daughter lies on her bed, the bed resting on the same floor boards as the bed of her grandmother. A book is open on her bed. The book lies open like a secret revealed; the book lying open over the bones of her grandmother.

Around the book transparent sheets, transparent hinges lie scattered. Inside the sheets: stamps. Stamps from foreign places, with codes and glyphs and symbols in foreign languages.

The girl picks up a crimson stamp in tweezers and places it carefully over the bones of her grandmother.

THE HORSESHOE

The younger daughter is pressed up against Mike Lazaroni inside his 1939 mandarin red Ford coupe. They are parked outside the girl's strange Mexican house on the curved dirt road known as the horseshoe. Somehow the red tile roof feels as if it is beneath the car. Everything feels atilt now that Mike Lazaroni has kissed the younger daughter, a wet exploratory kiss. When Mike Lazaroni leans back, a string of saliva glistens between them, then winks out like an imaginary star.

She has been kissed before. Terry Taylor never kissed her. But

Howard Mackey tried to kiss her every afternoon on their way up the steep footpath from Allesandro Street School. Every afternoon she would curl her hand into a fist and strike a blow that would last only until the next day. At junior high dances the clean blond boy with no personality never tries to kiss her. Wants only to dance, her hand resting on his soft neck.

Mike Lazaroni is different. Her mother has said so. More like a man, she says. Not just because he has his own car, paid for with money earned at the Texaco gas station. It is something else, something she can smell, like odors in the gym when boys play basketball. The hot burned scent of chiles roasting.

THE KITCHEN

Fourteen chiles lie in an even row releasing bacon fat into the folded paper towel. Over them, she smokes a cigarette. Then runs its smoldering head under a stream of tap water, drops the wetness into the kitchen trash, rinses her hands. Four sisters, all lying in bed on the sleeping porch, smoking. Still smoking, hiding the evidence, still moving under the watchful eyes of their mother, their mother always knowing.

She laughs companionably, whistles as she whips up the eggs: My funny valentine, sweet comic valentine. Flour onto the dish and cheese—where was it?—slicing into neat rectangles with her old dull knife, the one she hides under the dishtowels from her husband. Sweet comic valentine.

THE PATIO

Nestled as he has been inside the green velvet, the pain surprises, hacking his chest like a dull knife. He sits down. The reed case slips from his hand, the musician who cannot breathe. If he can lie down. In his bed. He enters by the side door. Nobody sees him.

THE MAID'S ROOM

Morocco, this one says. Sumatra. Tunisia. Caracas. Belize. She studies the art, the design, the style, the words of the stamps, the waving lines of cancellation. Por Avión, Mit Luftpost, By Air. She assembles, arranges, shapes, and fixes meaning in color, time, and place. Accomplishes movement by keeping still.

THE HORSESHOE

The younger daughter slams the door of Mike Lazaroni's mandarin red coupe and moves dreamily down the stairs of her Mexican house, past the cactus bed she tumbled into when she was three, past the slit in the wall saying *buzón*, down the patio steps toward the kitchen smelling of roasted chiles, where in a moment she will collide with her mother, who is saying with alarm and significance, "I can't wake your father."

She will know then—this daughter—and not know. She will know that she alone can wake him, and that she never can. She will know he is merely napping, and that he has already grown stiff, wrapped inside his prized *vicuña* skin from the Andes, that only a delicate line of saliva still connects his lip to this departing day.

IRON LUNG

The elder daughter is navigating her father's old Cadillac down Glendale Boulevard, her sister at her side. They are not weeping; they are having a theological conversation. Not until they are in their early forties, the age their mother is now, will they weep. They are on their way to make "the arrangements."

Two days ago when the mother said, "I can't wake your father," everything changed. The elder daughter became the elder son. The younger daughter became the mother. The mother took to her bed, turning into the child. The question, in a way, was: What had the father become?

By the father's own line of reasoning he had simply ceased to exist. Yet there had always been curious inconsistencies in his articulated belief system. The younger daughter, for example, has gathered from stray comments that though the father did not believe in God or in a hereafter, he did seem to think it possible that one might come back in the form of a sylph, a gnome, or a fairy.

The elder daughter, a Taurus, neither believes in such creatures nor that her father believed in them, though she does remember, will always remember in sharpest detail a flea circus she and her sister saw when they were nine and six that featured a formal wedding between two fleas, one in white gown, the other in a pearl gray tuxedo, an event her parents deny ever occurred.

This much is certain: Both girls clearly remember their father on numerous occasions expressing contempt for ritual, especially when it violated hygiene or common sense. It was his wish, when he died, to be quietly and sensibly cremated.

They are inclined, these daughters, to respect his wishes. The mother, however, who has withdrawn her support from the Catholic church because of the pope's refusal to acknowledge her marriage, seems nevertheless to have harbored some unarticulated remnant of belief. Though she lies apparently lifeless in her bed in a darkened room, her wishes nevertheless fill the back seat of the car. He must not be cremated. Otherwise she will not know where he is.

They turn right at the sign saying Forest Lawn. "The point is," says the elder sister, "that we must hold out for a pine box." Daughter of the First Consumer, she understands that life is economy and that power is understanding value. They must not be duped.

They park their father's car under a canopy of trees and make their way up a walk lined with naked cherubims and seraphims cast in marble. Everywhere are fountains and the sound of cascading water. At the door they are met by an oily gentleman in a charcoal gray suit who speaks in low tones and ushers them into a mahogany lined room with a fire burning in the hearth, though the day is warmish for February.

He understands their grief.

He does not, however, understand about the pine box.

First they will speak to the cosmetologist. The cosmetologist, they say? She settles on the chair in front of them with a clipboard. She tugs at her skirt. Her eyebrows arch like Joan Crawford's. She wants to know about his complexion. Where he parted his hair. If he wore scent. She is an artist, she explains. They will be pleased with her efforts. She will do him justice.

The oily man returns. They have three basic models, he explains. Models? Three lines of caskets. They study a brochure. He reminds them this is their last chance to do something really nice for their father.

Their thoughts turn instantly to cremation. They see a pyre in the desert, feel the heat of rising flames, join the dancing forms. They drum until the man stays their hands, offering to show them the caskets. Then they exchange glances, see together their mother lying on her bed with the blanket tucked tight around her, unmoving. They will look at the caskets.

There is a showroom of them. Row after row, with lids standing open, like hoods on new cars. Likewise, there are no prices in evidence. Starting at the top of the line is The Bronze. The lid is encrusted with decoration; the sides with heavy, ornate handles. Inside is rich satin and deep padding, as if for comfort. Something simpler, the older daughter says.

The Silver Line. A sort of brushed chrome. The difference, says the salesman, is—of course—the handles. The handles, they say? Next thing they know he is making a quick ratcheting sound and the long silver handle drops off in his hand. That way, he explains, we can pass the savings on to the customer. They stare at him. Well, we use them again, he explains.

He leads them to Basic. Basic is not even called a line. The handles are cheap, not worth keeping. Inside looks like the material used in Halloween costumes: flimsy witch cloth smelling of dye. The elder daughter asks again about the simple pine box. There are laws governing burial, after all, the man tells them.

They wander back to the Silver Line, pick one with deep green velvet like the lining of their father's reed case. They have just spent $1,657.49 of their father's money, not counting the limousine ($75), the hearse ($124), the two plots ($596), and the concrete vault with nonmetallic liner ($647). Ten miles away, their mother rolls over in her bed, sighs.

They return to the room with the fireplace. Two and a half hours have passed. They sit by the fire, waiting, staring into blazing gas flames. Then a woman comes in, leads them down another hall. They follow her like sleepwalkers. "This," she says flinging open a door, "is the Slumber Room."

She has a hard time making them understand. They keep asking questions that despite her patience and her professionalism begin to annoy. You put them in here, they say? Really? In the four poster bed? In their pajamas? Dead bodies in pajamas? With Muzak? Finally she hears herself say in a tone she hardly recognizes, "Look, your father was your mother's lover."

They look across the brocade bedspread and out the faceted window; they look seven hills away at their mother lying in her narrow bed, lying still, lying like a woman in an iron lung, not expected to live, watching them through angled mirrors.

TIME PASSES

In eighteen minutes it will be the day after the funeral. The elder sister lies in her father's Hollywood bed, propped up on one elbow, looking at her mother in the next bed. Moonlight enters like distant saxophone music through the open window next to the Singer sewing machine, insinuates itself through a little crack in the woven drapes. From time to time a breeze stirs the drapes, changing the patterns on the hardwood floor, shifting the filigree of moonlight.

The mother sighs. It is hard to tell if she is awake or asleep. She does not turn in her bed but remains outstretched, tucked in, assuming the shape of the casket she may or may not have seen lowered into the ground that afternoon.

The daughter lies back down in her father's bed, closes her eyes. She is not exactly asking for forgiveness; still she worries that parts of the funeral may have too closely resembled a flea circus. She echoes her mother's sigh.

The breeze stirs, sending moonlight in little explosions across the left toe of her father's shoe. He has been standing by the drapes, watching, listening to the sighing of his wife, sighing that sounds to him like waves on the shore of the country for which he must soon depart. He lingers now, having taken on the shape of the handsome twenty-four-year-old musician he has carried inside himself, curved like a saxophone, melodious. He listens to the sighing, no longer thinking about insurance, or burial rites, or the education of his daughters, or even about the network of roots under his Mexican house that every night multiply and creep into the intricacies of the plumbing, blocking all his designs. No, he is not thinking of this. He is simply taking thoughtful leave, like any traveler.

The younger daughter, sleeping alone in the maid's room at the opposite end of the house, stirs, hears something, footsteps on the four stairs leading up. She has been waiting for this. She remembers, or seems to remember, her father having said something about communication beyond the grave, something that made no sense if he really was an atheist, though Catherine has flatly said he was not. But Catherine is a Christian, belongs to the Salvation Army, wears a uniform sometimes. Jack was an agnostic, not an atheist, Catherine had said, and then burst into tears.

She herself has not cried. First she said she would cry after the ambulance took her father away, and then after Aunt Thelma got there, and then after making "the arrangements" with her sister, and then after the funeral, and then after she was in bed alone with the lights out and the door shut and nobody would see her or hear her, especially her mother.

Now she lies in her bed, listening to her father's footsteps coming up the stairs toward her room as he has done so many times before, bearing once a cardboard fireman's hat, bearing often a sack of crab claws; sees him pause in the doorway, backlit from the fluorescent light over the kitchen sink. He is a young man not much older than Mike Lazaroni, his hair carefully combed back, his face simple and sophisticated. He is dressed in tails, like Fred Astaire. In his hand is the alto saxophone that rests in her own closet next to the baseball bat.

"Daddy?" she says. He smiles at her, places his index finger perpendicular against his lips in a conspiratorial sign of silence, pauses, then backs out, leaving the door ajar.

A light breeze swirls a nest of leaves across the patio outside her bathroom window. Over the house a vault of stars arches. She wishes the stars would rise and fall, rise and fall three hundred and sixty-five times so that a whole year will have passed by the time morning comes, so that her mother can split open the cocoon in which she sleeps, so that she can unfold and emerge whole and entire and take up the business of being her mother again. And she wishes this so intently, lying under the tile roof in her father's house, wishes it with the deep and serious intent of a young writer, an artist, dreaming her way toward actuality, that in fact, when the family wakes, each of them stretching and blinking her way toward the morning, a full year has passed.

THE WINDOW

Clara Ignacia Ríos is sitting in the kitchen of the Oxnard Inn putting on her brother's boots. Her feet, inside the three pair of socks, feel cut off, without sensation, as if they are thick loaves made from the dough her mother is rolling out on the table behind her. Sleepily she hears the rumble of the rolling pin over the dough, the click, click of Grace Ann's potato peeler flying over the potatoes piling up slowly in the hotel sink. Grace Ann has rollers in her hair even though it is against the rules and is Wednesday besides.

Clara laces the boots very tight and double knots them at the top. She is wearing her waitress uniform, which has short sleeves and a tiny starched apron sewed stupidly right onto the skirt. Clara hates this uniform and this job, hates Oxnard too, and the double-wide trailer, and her brother, who by rights should be taking this wood to the cottages himself since her father is too sick to do it.

She squints out the western window, across the porch, the smooth expanse of sand, the sea rising and falling like a gentle pulse inside a drowsy woman, everything gone purple in the dawning.

Her mother puts a thick white mug of coffee into her hand, says "mi'ja," in that way she has, turns back to the rolling of the dough.

Grace Ann is peeling potatoes ruefully, saying the woman in the north cottage is lucky to be a widow and rich too. Clara sips her coffee, waits for her mother to caution Grace Ann about talking in such a way. Then she reaches her father's thick jacket off the peg by the door and zips it up to her chin. She stomps her feet experimentally and looks down, down at the pink skirt dangling beneath the smudgy jacket, the boots encasing her lost feet.

"If you ask me . . ." says Grace Ann. Clara opens the back door and steps out onto the porch, pulls the door tight against the tiresome voice. The wind from the north whips up her skirt, inflates it like a sail she beats back. By the time she gets to the bottom step, she hears the kitchen door open and her mother is flinging down her father's knit cap to her. "Put that on, mi'ja," she says, and slams the door shut again, against the wind.

One day Clara will leave this place, where the wind howls day and night. She will go to Mexico City and study art. She will never marry. She will have her own house by the sea, where the wind is gentle, and all the clothes that she wears will be her own.

She stops at the woodpile and fills her arms with the logs. She can carry as many as her brother and more than her father. She starts out across the sand toward the north cottage, the farthest away, the one where the widow and her daughters sleep.

Her father has seen them. On the beach. "The beautiful señora," he calls the woman when Clara's mother is not near. "The beautiful señora sits on a fallen oak, drawing with a green pencil. Her eldest daughter, guapa too, the one with the dark hair, la morena, drawing also, but with a hundred colored pencils kept in a tin box. La otra, the younger, has freckles on her nose, stands in the freezing water, staring out to sea. Or she runs along the beach like a wild thing."

Clara steps toward the north cottage, bearing wood for them, trying to remember the strange book her English teacher at the junior college gave her to read: *Little Women*. That was it. *Little Women*. Marmie, Beth, Jo. Others, but she could not remember their names. A large house filled with girls. Only girls. And the father had died too, like theirs, had he not? There had been something about the war and men going off and the women staying home knitting stockings and mending clothes and worrying about the men and about money. Perhaps these women are not rich after all.

Clara has passed two cottages nearer the inn. Both empty. Now the north cottage, and it too dark, though she thinks she saw a wisp of smoke coming from the chimney. She stacks the wood by the door. Quietly. Her brother would have thrown the wood against the house in hopes the women would wake up and praise him for doing what was only his job. For a moment, as she stands shivering, and breathing, she half hopes they *will* hear her and invite her into the warm parlor where Marmie will be knitting and the girls drinking cocoa.

Clara walks quietly around to the side window and looks inside. On each of the two day beds there is a rumple of sheets and blankets. Against the far wall Clara can just make out on the pillow a swirl of shining dark hair. *La morena.* Hair that looks as soft as a bird's wing, and for a moment Clara can almost feel it against her hand, as if she is there, standing over the sleeping girl, gently stroking that hair, that wing of a bird.

As she stands there—one of her selves outside in the wind, the other self inside breathing in time with this older daughter—she feels someone watching her watching, and for a minute does not know whether the watcher is inside or outside. It is the other girl, *la otra,* she with the freckles, raised up in the dark on one elbow. Regarding her. Looking, looking until at last Clara disappears from the window.

MILAGRITOS

The girl stands with her hands in her pockets, the waters of the Gulf of California pooled around her ankles like some warm bathtub. She did not expect this, the warmth, the stillness. That chill Pacific has been her god. Her goddess. *Océano,* she would murmur, letting the cold drag her into the waves, letting it sink her deeper and deeper into the sand.

But this. Was different. She did not know whose god this was. So she stands waiting, hands in pockets on this warm evening in Guaymas watching the Mexican sun slip toward inscrutable waters.

Inscrutable, she says. Out loud. Then looks to see if anybody has heard. Nobody on her left; on her right the man in rolled up jeans fishing for shark. Her sister is back at the hotel reading *Wuthering Heights.* Behind her, her mother sits on the seawall smoking Pall Malls, while tourists clatter by in carriages drawn by horses.

She did this, her mother. Brought her to the ocean. Would drive her down Sunset Boulevard, miles, parking the car in the lot at Will Rogers State Beach. Would sit there. Smoking. Sometimes running the engine, the heater, for warmth, while her daughter walked miles, musing, thrumming, singing, wailing. Not liking the beach herself, for it was dirty. People sitting in dirt, though her own mother had loved it, would pack up the thirteen children and take them to Will Rogers, camp for a week, cooking over a fire, sitting in a canvas chair wearing her black dress with the small white polka dots, her black straw hat. Hot black leather shoes. And then the granddaughter, walking the same beach as if her life depended on it.

Inscrutable the girl says half-aloud, her mother. Smoking her
cigarettes on a beach in Mexico. Hating sand. Not alarmed, really,

when the man in the rolled up pants had said he was fishing for shark. Would sit smoking while her daughter waded in shark-infested waters.

The Mexican sun has slipped closer now, moving toward her lover. And the girl wonders, for the first time perhaps, if she has brought her mother here, or if her mother has brought her here. She cannot remember, really, how this decision came about.

She remembers their selling the house, remembers the two men her mother introduced, the "couple" Catherine had called them. The men her mother had found in less than a week when her father had spent a whole lifetime putting the house on and taking it off the market. Her mother, who had never written a check in her life.

She remembers high school and falling in love twice. Perhaps more. No—she corrects herself—twice. Once with her English teacher and once with the French. Is in love with them still. Both. One a woman; one a man. She stands now with her two feet planted in the Gulf of California, the two sides of her ample heart devoted and dedicated, one side to the beautiful middle-aged, henna-haired former dancer and the other to the very young man in the charcoal gray, three-piece suit, the man with the pale, slender wrists. And for a moment she hangs—like the sun on the verge of immersion—on the verge of tears.

No. She will not cry. But she thinks of the church in Hermosillo where they stopped for lunch and of the saint who had a little glass case in her ceramic chest right where her heart should have been. A glass case divided down the middle. On one side was Mary and on the other was Jesus. She could see inside her own heart now, divided this same way, left and right, woman and man. Mary the henna-haired dancer; Jesus the pale scholar with slim wrists. Both lost: the loves of her life.

She turns to her mother, smoking in the last light, turns back to the slipping sun. She remembers graduating, she thinks of the pink typewriter her mother gave her, a pink Smith Corona with white keys that she must have ordered because who ever saw a pink typewriter? (Her mother could not abide practical gifts.) The pink typewriter is in the trunk of the Buick, she remembers, but she does not remember ever sitting down—the three of them— and deciding to sell everything and move to Mexico.

And now that she says it, almost out loud, she realizes how familiar these words are: Sell everything and move to Mexico. She has grown up in an atmosphere of impending journey, has grown up with those words woven together with a certain inevitability as if once you say "sell everything" you must say "and move to Mexico." Then are they here (she moves her toes in the warmth of the Gulf) precisely because of the inevitability of these phrases snapping together like two magnets? In short, are they here because of her father's dream?

No. Unthinkable. Her mother does not do things in this way. Her mother simply does things. Her mother's way is to sit on the wall smoking while others dream.

In this way she keeps us from harm.

OVERHEARD AT THE REFORMA

Though it is summer and hot in Mexico City my mother has a fur boa around her neck and looks a lot like Ava Gardner. We are sitting in the bar of the Reforma Hotel having margaritas and feeling excited, waiting for friends. This is what happens. We are talking and laughing when all at once we get quiet because we are all eavesdropping on the two men sitting in the booth behind us. They are talking about my mother. In Spanish.

I listen hard, bringing to bear everything I learned about Spanish in Mymama's kitchen and in Mrs. Olrich's classes for four long years. Still there are certain things Mrs. Olrich left out, like anything having to do with the body, whether on the most basic or the most sublime level. In short I could neither ask where the bathroom was nor speak to anybody in the familiar form. Mrs. Olrich said she could not conceive why we would ever need to utter the word *tu*.

Therefore I am listening intently to add to my vocabulary and because *las paredes oyen*. These men are saying how beautiful and *delicada* and *deliciosa mi madre es*. In fact it sounds like they are speaking in the subjunctive, which I think of as the tense of intense longing.

When I look over at my mother I see that she has understood them, these men in their admiration. Every single word. My mother, who never could remember how to pronounce *hay* during my father's nightly Spanish lessons, now understood *cada palabra*.

Will she learn to speak it too? *¡Ojalá!*

You've seen these. Nightclub photographs taken under duress. We are at El Patio, where my mother has assembled us: the three of us, and also my best friend from high school, Betty Lou Feinstein, her mother Bertha Feinstein, and my aunt, Crazy Rena, who have all flown down from Los Angeles. Dead center is the table and we are arranged around it, almost like a family dinner. Except everybody is well-dressed and our expressions are mostly glazed.

PHOTOGRAPH 9

Noticeable in this respect is Betty Lou. Think of her as Chabela, which is the name Mrs. Olrich gave her in Spanish Club. Chabelita is definitely not amused. She sits on the left with her long legs crossed in the foreground, like a warning sign. The flashbulb has illuminated these long legs and reflects in her mother's decorative glasses opposite. It is Chabela's life's work not to become her mother, who according to her daughter has a mercantile mind. For this mother, however, it is clear that being at a nightclub called El Patio in Mexico City represents the apex of her life. For Chabelita it is the nadir. Chabelita's right arm is bent, resting on the back of her chair, supporting the languid hand that holds her seventeenth cigarette of the evening.

Behind her sits Crazy Rena, whose nervous hands clutch her purse in her lap. A white glove is arrested in its slide toward the floor and her bitten nails are polished and ready. There is a slight cast to her left eye. Either that or she is eyeing the handsome waiter over her left shoulder.

My sister sits opposite Chabelita, and she is in her Audrey Hepburn mode, the way—to be honest—my mother likes her best. Her hair is shiny and softly curled; she wears makeup. The earrings have stolen, nevertheless, from her earlobes into the beaded bag in her lap, and her left foot is easing the tight but

stylish pump off her right. She is smiling in an open way, as if
she believes we will all survive this.

Next to her, with Bertha on my right, I sit, staring obliquely
at some indistinct spot in the foreground. My hair is short,
my shoulders bare, my smile deflected.

The only person looking directly into the camera is my
mother. Her slender and penciled eyebrows arch as if in delighted
surprise. A flower perches in her long, coiled hair; a fur slips per-
petually, tantalizingly off her right shoulder. A corpulent man in
white dinner jacket at the table behind ours seems poised, as if
to rescue the fur, to somehow act, a stranger brought into this
family photo all unbeknownst.

DINNER 1957

When it storms in Mexico City the lights go out. That's why finding their cousin's house was difficult. The elder daughter held the map under the dome light while the mother drove. The younger daughter, who inclined to car sickness and a poor sense of direction, sat in the back seat with the window rolled down.

When they stopped at last, still they were unsure. A strange city. A cousin whom only the mother had met, years ago in Texas, the daughter of her husband's brother. The girls hardly knew this side of the family. They knew their mother's family. But here they were, in search of Dolores, their father's niece.

The younger daughter knew *dolores* meant pains. Yet the younger daughter knew also that Dolores was the eldest daughter of her Aunt Una. The younger daughter knew that *una* meant *one*. Besides, she was hungry.

When they knocked on the door it seemed to open on emptiness, so short was their cousin. The next thing they knew they were clasped to the bosom of a laughing woman, a dark, corpulent, rollicking woman whose name had failed to describe her, who could hug them and balance a flickering candle all at the same time.

They ate by candlelight. A delicious cold supper. No electricity, of course. Her husband was at their country house in Tepotzlán, working on a book, was sorry not to be there to meet them. Tepotzlán, a beautiful village just south of the city; they must all come for the long weekend. The maid here in the city had left just yesterday, taking the appliances with her. Also bracelets, rings, brooches. All gone, this cousin named Dolores laughed. And you couldn't call the police because they would take whatever was left. As everybody knew.

Later they sat in the living room, watching the face of their cousin, watching her plump hands move through the air, conjuring stories in the flickering light. These travelers.

INVENTORY

The sisters have arranged and rearranged the luggage three times and still Pancho Villa's feet stick out the rear window.

Yesterday in the marketplace their last afternoon before their aunt, the younger daughter's high school friend, and the friend's mother flew back to Los Angeles it had seemed simple enough. The car was, after all, big. A charcoal gray Buick Century with red upholstery and wire wheels that their mother had purchased against the advice of *Consumer's Report,* who—along with the daughters—recommended the economy of a VW bug. Since it had seemed essential to their mother to purchase such a vulgar car, they might as well use it.

Now, struggling in the underground parking lot of the Reforma Hotel with a six-foot straw Pancho Villa, they became aware—though they did not mention it—of a curious reversal. Whereas since adolescence they had disapproved of their mother's habits of acquisition, thinking of themselves as soldiers of fortune, traveling light, ready for anything, they now began to perceive it was their mother who was traveling light (one suitcase and a cosmetic case) and they who were acquiring and accumulating. In addition to a suitcase apiece, the elder sister had collected a fragile but colorful ceramic tree of life (packed carefully in mountains of shredded newspaper), two pair of sandals, handmade Mexican art paper (to be carried flat), and a papier-mâché blond doll with movable arms and legs (dressed as an acrobat). The younger sister had six handmade demitasse cups (of surprising irregularity), a set of silver salad servers with rosewood handles, six hand-blown blue glasses, and a copy of *Don Quijote* in Spanish.

While it was true the elder sister had not insisted on purchasing Pancho Villa's matching horse—tempted though she was—nevertheless Pancho Villa himself had seemed necessary. Yesterday, standing in the marketplace alone together, the two sisters had agreed he was "magnificent," with his great height, his twin holsters and pistols, his twin ammunition belts crossing his manly chest, his broad sombrero, and his cowboy boots furnished with raffish spurs. Now they felt a little weakened with the exertion and with *la turista,* which had dogged their steps almost from the first day. Their mother's health had never been better.

By the time she emerged smiling and easy from the elevator, excited about their weekend trip to visit cousin Dolores in Tepotzlán, her daughters had jammed everything into the Buick's trunk and halfway across the back seat. The younger daughter sat in the back seat on plush red upholstery, the gigantic body of Villa wedging her in but not obscuring the view of her mother holding out her open hand to the elevator operator so he could negotiate his own tip. There was certainly no mystery about Mexican currency, but still she persisted in holding out her hand and letting people just help themselves.

She slid behind the wheel. Put it in neutral. Turned the key. As if nobody else knew how to drive; as if nobody else had been licensed by the state of California for almost two years.

The map to Tepotzlán was in her purse. The elder sister dug through, brought up a Reforma cocktail napkin with a map drawn in eyebrow pencil. At the parking attendant's booth they stopped, the mother holding out a handful of coins, then they shoot forth into Mexican sun.

Book Three

It was not far, Dolores had told them, not far to their house in the country. A little south of the city. But really, who knows? Distance in Mexico flashes sudden and long, like the tongue of a lizard. Then closes like the lizard eye, a slow line traveling down.

When she woke, the younger daughter was hot. She was thirsty. She was tired of Pancho Villa's body at odds with her own. She was tired of traveling. She was tired of carrying around the little glass cage of a heart split in two and divided between her loves: the English teacher and the French teacher; Mary and Christ; the female and the male; the forbidden and the conventional. So much drama and dichotomy. When would she have either succor or solitude?

She wadded up her sweater under her head but she was not comfortable. She closed her eyes, saw herself unpacking the blue hand-blown glasses, wiping them clean, setting two out on a round table in a garage apartment in Iowa City. She had only seen blue like this in the fragile eyes of her French teacher, whom it seemed she must marry. But running her hand down the rosewood handle on a silver spoon she saw the hennaed hair of her English teacher, with whom eventually she must run away.

When her mother asked her suddenly and unexpectedly if she would like to drive, she could hardly speak, as if her mother had seen through the trunk to the box containing the glassware and the cups and the silver spoons and knew their meaning far better than she herself did. Her mother carefully pulled the car to the side of the road, and they changed places.

MOVING PICTURES

It is raining in the village of Tepotzlán. Water glistens on the broad leaves and flows in sheets down the terraced stone street. Nobody is out in weather like this. The few buildings, side by side, look blind, as if they have turned within.

Only Amalia Jerez, sweeping out El Cine Real (for it is Saturday night), sweeping with the door open, sees the great car approaching, the color of rain itself, moving carefully between the buildings with the grace of a fat man dancing. She scarcely knows how it is not scraping on both sides, it is that wide. And as she watches and listens, it comes to the first terrace—almost opposite—and starts down, giving at first a groaning sound from its belly; then levels out, moving toward the next terrace. And as it drags itself in line with her eye—though the rain is coming harder now—she sees them. Sticking out of the window, the boots of a dead man! Slowly and in wonder she crosses herself twice, murmurs "Ay, dios mío," watches as the car carries the man to the next level, then disappears down into the rain.

TEPOTZLÁN

It takes a long time, struggling in the dark, rain dripping off Dolores's roof onto our heads, to get that straw man out of the back seat. He resists us. From under the eaves, Mother keeps calling through the sheet of rain, "Leave him. Leave him for later."

But we are not going to do that, my sister and I. Finally we roll down the rear window and pull him out, feet first. We run toward the house with him, his body swinging between us. Our cousin holds the door open. "Déjelo aquí," she says. We lean him against the wall and are grabbed and held in damp hugs and kisses.

My mother looks at the puddles forming on the tiles around his wet boots. "He smells," she says, setting her cosmetic case down in exhaustion.

"Oh, but he's magnificent," says Dolores, staring up into his face. In the dim light I can't quite tell, but it feels like she rocks up on her toes, short as she is, leaning toward him for a better look. Or maybe to kiss him, I think strangely. I don't know why. Just then the generator cycles off and the lights go way down, almost off, and when they come up again Dolores is just standing there, all level again, with her hands in her apron pockets, saying, "Simply magnificent."

That night we climb into narrow beds, clean sheets slightly damp. My sister and I have a room to ourselves. In the dark we shiver and talk. About the truck filled with boys who sang about "La Llorona" and played guitars. About the woman at dinner who only comes to Tepotzlán for the summers and for the rest of the year gives her beautiful house to an artist who will care for it. There is a studio and a swimming pool and a lazy cat. One day we will come back together as caretakers, my sister to paint, I to write. We promise each other.

The generator clicks on and off as we talk, laying our plans. Across the courtyard we can hear the gardener and the maid— husband and wife—in argument, then the voice of Dolores rising over theirs, weaving domestic discord in with the sounds of rain drumming on thick leaves, the bark of a dog, the call of a tropical bird, the rush of the stream past our bedroom window.

In this house under the stars we will fall asleep, dreaming the past into tropes and signs and symbols, beginning the dangerous art of fitting it all back inside the heart of a child.

ART CATALOGUE

LA VÍA

Stepping Out
16 1/4" X 7" X 3 3/4" (art); 19" X 7 1/2" X 4 1/2" (plexi case). Mixed media. 1995.

Waiting for the Red Car
10 3/4" X 8" X 2 5/8" (art); 11 3/4 X 9 1/4" x 4" (plexi case). Mixed media. 1992.

Family Room
5 1/2" X 13 1/2" X 4". Mixed media. 1992.

El Músico y la Dama.
13 3/4" X 11" X 4" (closed); 13 3/4" X 22" X 3" (open). Mixed media. 1995.

Pocadillas
6 5/8" X 7 3/4". Mixed media. 1991.

Cowgirls Don't Wear White Gloves
5 1/2" X 11 1/4" X 4 1/2" (open). Mixed media. 1995.

Winifred, Her Story.
14" X 10" X 8" (open). Mixed media. 1993.

My Mama's Mexi-Briefcase.
1 1/2" X 10 3/4" X 10 3/4" (closed); 11 1/2" X 10 3/4" X 10 3/4" (open). Mixed media. 1995.

Texas Two-Step/History of a Self-made Man.
11" X 18" X 8 1/2" (closed); 8 1/2" X 18" X 13" (open). Mixed media. 1995.

"You Think Too Much"
9 1/4" X 6" X 3 1/2" (closed); 9 1/4" X 10" X 10"(open). Mixed media. 1990.

LA GALERÍA

Girl's Dream
13" X 3.5" (art); 15.5" X 4.5" X 4.5" (plexi case). Mixed media. 1990.

Homage to a Tree House
12 3/4" X 8" X 7" (lights). Mixed media. 1994.

Night Closet
8 1/2" X 4 3/8" X 2 3/4" (art); 14" X 9 3/4" (plexi wall hung). Mixed media. 1991.

Good Dog/Bad Dog
14 1/2" X 10" X 6 1/2" (lights). Mixed media. 1995.

Recuerdos Para Los Abuelitos
16" X 18" X 9" (open) Mixed media. 1994.

Catch the Wave
9 1/2" X 8" X 2" (art); 10 1/2" X 10" X 4" (plexi case). Mixed media. 1992.

Fly Away
8 1/2" X 8" X 1 1/2" (art); 10" x 8 1/2" X 3" (plexi case). Mixed media. 1992.

House of Pictures
6" X 19" X 11 3/4" (closed); 16" X 19" X 16" (open). Mixed media. 1995.

Ofrenda for a Maja
13" X 23 1/2" X 5 3/4" (open). Mixed media. 1994.

Pelorus
15" X 12" X 15 1/2". Mixed media. 1995.

Photos by Philip Cohen, Oakland, California